Mommy Rescue Guide

Welcome to the lifesaving *Mommy Rescue Guide* series! Each *Mommy Rescue Guide* offers techniques and advice written by recognized parenting authorities.

These engaging, informative books give you the help you need when you need it the most! The *Mommy Rescue Guides* are quick, issue-specific, and easy to carry anywhere and everywhere.

You can read one from cover to cover or just pick out the information you need for rapid relief! Whether you're in a bind or you have some time, these books will make being a mom painless and fun!

Being a good mom has never been easier!

Contents

Introduction

GOOD NEWS—temper tantrums are normal! Every mommy can expect to encounter at least a few meltdowns as their child grows. And although temper tantrums are often frustrating and upsetting, they are as common as skinned knees, muddy shoes, lost game pieces, bogeyman fears, and all of the other day-to-day challenges of raising a child.

The popular notion these days is that all children are motivated to have temper tantrums just for attention. The most common responses advocated are: give in, punish, or ignore. If only it was that simple! The truth is that there are many possible reasons for your child's temper tantrums.

Your child is a complex and unique individual and their behavior cannot be explained by a one-size-fits-all, cookie cutter approach. Give in, punish, or ignore? There must be more! And there is. The ideas and suggestions in *Mommy Rescue Guide: Tantrums* go way beyond a "quick fix." Yes, you will find specific real-life strategies for responding and coping with your child's temper tantrums and emotional outbursts and you will find ways to help your child develop self-control as well.

This book will be your guide as your child grows. You will read about the common causes for temper tantrums for each stage of your child's development. You will find coping strategies that are appropriate and relevant, based on the cause of your child's temper tantrum.

Inside this book, you will also find advice on preventing temper tantrums, how to manage temper tantrums in special situations, and when to worry about your child's behavior. You will also discover simple and fun activities that will not only help diminish your child's temper tantrums but will also teach them social, emotional, and cognitive skills that they will use for a lifetime!

Chapter 1

The Truth About Temper Tantrums

Do you know how to handle your child when she's crying, kicking and screaming, and having a melt down? No? Sometimes? Never? Well you're not alone! Everyday, everywhere, moms face tantrums and struggle to know what to do about it! The first step is to understand what a temper tantrum is and what causes it. This is half the battle in dealing with it. After you understand your child's behavior, you can try to change it. In this chapter, you will learn about what you can expect from your child's behavior throughout different age groups and stages.

Blues or Bliss? Your Child's Behavior

A temper tantrum is essentially an uncontrolled outburst of emotion. Temper tantrums are sometimes referred to as fits or meltdowns, and are a common behavior during childhood. Temper tantrums are especially common between the ages of two and four and are seen routinely in about 80 percent of all children. Temper tantrums may include verbal outbursts, physical outbursts, or both. Temper tantrum behavior will be different for every child. Additionally, you can expect to see your child's tantrum behavior change as she grows. Common behaviors include crying and screaming, kicking, pouting, and hitting. These outbursts are generally quite intense, but fortunately, they do not last long. In fact, most temper tantrums begin to subside within the first minute and rarely last longer than five or ten minutes.

What's Common, What's Not?

The way that each child behaves when she has a temper tantrum is as unique as she is. The truth is, there is not any typical or atypical temper tantrum behavior. Each child is different and tantrums are influenced by the age of the child. There will be times when your toddler is so emotionally distraught that you will be unable to determine what has caused this latest meltdown. Then, when your child reaches preschool, he has some verbal skills for expressing his emotion, which sometimes makes things more challenging.

Below, parents share with you some of their experiences with tantrums. None of these examples is unusual, and perhaps you will see a bit of your own child in each them! Let's take a look:

"When my son was about two years old, he was overtired and one night he just had a meltdown. I remember him running around the house crying and screaming. At one point he picked up one of those Rubbermaid step stools and whacked himself in the head with it!"

Jamie B.

"When my daughter was about fifteen months, we went to one of the state parks in our area, and went swimming at the beach. When it was time to leave, my daughter had a major meltdown because she did not want to go. I would put her in the stroller, and she would climb out—undo the buckle and everything! I ended up carrying her to the car. She kept blocking me from buckling her in. Finally I got her in the car seat, and she was still crying and screaming. I drove most of the way home with her like that, until she just conked out and slept."

Jill B.

"We went to a local mall, and we were in the toy store. My two-year-old daughter started throwing a fit about wanting something. My husband and I both told her no and that if she did not stop, we were leaving. She did not stop. My husband was not done shopping, so I got the joy of carrying her through the mall to the exit. She was kicking and screaming the entire time."

Sharon D.

"One night, my son was so distraught because I left to go for a walk, that he waited by the front door for me. Well, my husband called me, as I had my cell phone, and told me that I had to come in the back door. Here my son had cried while he sat in the box we have for shoes at the front door and he eventually cried himself to sleep in the box!"

Tanya.

"My daughter's worst temper tantrums are now peaking at age four. Before now, she usually just got mad. I would set her in her room, and tell her to come out when she felt like she could calm down and talk about it. Now I take her to her room, shut the door, and she bangs on the door, throws things around, and yells, 'Let me out of here. Open the door? Aaarrrgggh!' and so on. Repeatedly. And 90 percent of the time, it lasts about five minutes straight, and I will go in to find her asleep. She will try to tell me 'grown-ups are supposed to let kids do what they want. If you make me go in my room, I will scream and cry because I am not happy.' Most of her fits are about not getting to watch TV. That is her one hot button at four. Before this age, it was about fights with her friends. Now she's doing really well with playing nicely and sharing."

Michelle K.

"My four-year-old is bossy to all the kids and she is downright demanding to me. Her tantrums are wild. We are at battle every day. It is so tiring. A lot *of times I want to just give in and let her have her way just so there isn't a constant fight. It seems that as soon as she has been turned down for one thing, she instantly thinks of the next thing that I will say no to. It makes me think she is intentionally looking for negative attention."*

Belle R.

"My daughter is three and no matter what I say to her or how I say it, she has to say no. She always puts up a fight, and when she does not get what she wants, she starts to shriek."

Maria G.

If You Have a Toddler . . .

They don't call it the "terrible twos" for nothing! The toddler years are prime time for temper tantrums. Some parents report that their children began having temper tantrums as early as one year of age. However, tantrum behavior is not very common until the child is two years old. It is believed that as many as 20 percent of all two- and three-year-olds will have more than two temper tantrums a day.

Because your toddler does not possess much self-control, his temper tantrums are likely to be very intense. Once he becomes emotionally worked up, he may have a hard time calming down and regaining control. Children will have their own unique way

5

•

of throwing a tantrum. You may see your toddler cry, hit, throw himself to the ground, screech, flail, or kick when he has a tantrum.

It's important to remember that toddlers do not have temper tantrums out of spite! There are some common reasons for toddler temper tantrums. Let's take a close look at each of these triggers.

Separation Anxiety

Although you may witness your child having a temper tantrum when you leave when she is as young as ten months of age, separation anxiety usually reaches its peak around age two and a half years. If your child has separation anxiety, she may be very clingy and may throw a tantrum whenever you try to leave her. Children with secure attachments do tend to have less difficulty with separation.

Egocentrism

When your child is egocentric, she will have a hard time seeing and understanding someone else's perspective, and will think the world revolves around her. This results in temper tantrums about possession and sharing. Being egocentric also makes it difficult

Mindful Mommy

Your toddler's temper tantrums are not planned or intentional. There are many reasons why your toddler may have a temper tantrum, but all of the reasons stem from either environmental factors such as over-stimulation or fatigue or from the natural development of your child's cognitive, social, and emotional maturity.

for children to negotiate and resolve conflicts with others, because they can see only their own point of view.

Autonomy

During the second and third years of his life, your child may begin to engage you in power struggles and display negativity as he starts to assert his growing independence and identity.

Lack of Language Skills

Without language skills, your toddler has limited ways to express her strong emotions. Unable to verbalize her frustration, she is more likely to lash out physically or burst into tears. Aggressive behaviors usually will diminish once a child acquires adequate language skills to use for conflict resolution.

If You Have a Preschooler . . .

Although it is likely that your child will have temper tantrums through the preschool years, you should notice a decrease in frequency from the toddler years. Only about 10 percent of preschoolers will have more than two temper tantrums a day.

By the time he's in preschool, your child has acquired some ability to use language and to recognize and manage his emotions. Therefore, the intensity of his temper tantrum behavior will diminish. However, your child is still prone to strong feelings of anger and frustration. When your preschooler has a temper tantrum, you may see him throw things, hold his breath, stomp, yell, or whine. Indeed, strong emotions can still play havoc with your preschool-aged child's self-control. Your preschooler may still have temper tantrums because of separation anxiety and egocentrism.

It's Only a Matter of Time . . .

Your preschooler still does not understand time concepts. She will have a hard time being patient and delaying gratification. When she wants something, she wants it now! Learning impulse control and patience to wait is a skill that your child will need to work on throughout her preschool years.

I Want to Be a Big Kid!

Your child is acquiring many new motor, social, and cognitive skills. He has a need to feel competent and successful and, therefore, he often experiences frustration trying to do as well as the "big kids." The more he tries to master new skills and adventures, the more times he's bound to experience some failure. Young children need to learn to persevere and resist frustration.

Pay Attention to Me!

If you have been quick to respond to her pleas for rule changes, toys, and so forth by giving in to her demands, your child may begin to intentionally engage in tantrum behavior solely for the purpose of getting attention or something else that she wants. Temper tantrums can be a method either of getting the attention they truly need or of manipulation.

If You Have a School-Aged Child . . .

By the time your child enters school, temper tantrums will be less frequent; however, the occasional tantrums your child does have will still be troubling. When your school-aged child has a temper tantrum, it is unlikely he will flail about on the ground kicking and screaming. Rather, he may become defiant, sulk, swear, or become aggressive or destructive. These behaviors require a new mommy-mindset and even more patience.

Your school-aged child has acquired a level of emotional maturity that should help her delay gratification and tolerate frustration more easily. Her improved cognitive abilities mean that she's no longer egocentric, and that she has a rudimentary sense of right and wrong. However, there may be times when children this age still have difficulty managing their stronger feelings. They are most prone to having temper

Mommy Knows Best

Generally, aggression, along with temper tantrum behavior, will decrease as your child matures. Instrumental aggression peaks at ages two and three and even intentional aggression usually declines by the age of eight.

9

tantrums when there is a major change or stressful event in their life, such as a death in the family or the family's moving to a new town.

There are some common reasons why your school-aged child may still have a temper tantrum. Your child may still resort to tantrum behavior if she has learned that this is an effective way to get what she wants. Manipulation temper tantrums may increase as your child ages. When your child enters school, her social relationships expand. Along with many newfound friends, your child may face struggles with teasing, social isolation, and peer pressure. As your school-ager struggles to become more competent and independent, you may see an increase in defiance and power struggles as she begins to question your wisdom and authority

Is Your Child Afraid?

One strong emotion that may become particularly troubling for both toddlers and preschoolers is fear. For some children, strong fears and anxieties may result in a temper tantrum. Again, temper tantrum behavior may be the way that they deal with this strong emotion. Extreme fear will evoke an instinctive fight-or-flight response in your child. When confronted with something that is scary, your child may try to run, or he may resort to screaming and kicking. He will do whatever he can to avoid what he fears.

Don't Be Silly!

Respond to your child's fears with empathy and patience. Even her illogical fears feel very real to her. Avoid ridicule or punishment, as that will only serve to increase your child's anxiety. Allow your child to approach what she is frightened of at her own pace. You can help her cope with fear by reassuring her and giving her some control over the situation. You can do this by saying,

> "I promise that I will keep you safe at the circus. I know that the clowns frighten you. Where do you feel is a safe and comfortable place to sit?"

After a while, you might say something like,

> "We have been sitting very far away from the clowns. We have seen that they are silly and friendly. Do you think that you are ready to move a little bit closer?"

Read All About It

You may also wish to share some of the many picture books about dealing with fears. Sharing a story

Mindful Mommy

Because preschoolers do not yet have the cognitive skills to understand the difference between fact and fantasy, they will often become afraid of irrational or fictional things. Fears of the bogeyman, monsters, clowns, witches, and so forth are common during this time of your child's development.

is a safe way to talk about what is frightening for your child. Through the story, your child will be able to see how other children have learned to manage their fears. A good book to start with is *There's a Nightmare in My Closet*, by Mercer Mayer.

Take Action

Some parents discover that they can help their child conquer a fear by joining the child and taking imaginary action against the fear. This seems to work particularly well against fictional monsters, ghosts, bogeymen, and the like. Here are some ideas:

- Use a room deodorizer can to spray "monster repellent" in the closet. The fragrance can be tangible evidence.
- Go through the actions of locking the ghost up in a chest or box.
- Try asking your child to make a picture of what she is afraid of and then have her rip up the picture and throw it away or flush it down the toilet in a symbolic gesture.
- Assign a teddy bear or doll to stand watch over her if she is scared at night.

Mommy Knows Best

Children learn through imitation. Your young toddler or preschooler will be aware of your fears and apprehensions. If they witness that you are afraid of something, they will be likely to be scared as well, even if they have never had direct exposure to what frightens you.

Tantrum Myths Revealed

For most parents, parenting knowledge comes from two main sources: how they were raised and common knowledge gleaned from media and the advice of other well-meaning people. Some of this information will be useful, but at times, it may be based on outmoded views, different beliefs, and even faulty research. Not all of what you have heard about temper tantrums may be true. And not all of it applies to you and your family! Let's look at some common beliefs and get to the truth of the matter:

Temper Tantrums Are Unhealthy

Wrong. Not only are temper tantrums normal, but also they serve a healthy purpose. For young children with limited language skills, these outbursts are often the only way to communicate their needs. In addition, temper tantrums provide your child with a much-needed outlet to vent their strong emotions of anger and frustration.

A Temper Tantrum–Prone Child Is a Bad Child

Wrong. Temper tantrums are not bad, and neither

Mommy Knows Best

You will surely receive a lot of advice on parenting and disciplining your child from well-meaning friends and family members. Some advice, indeed, will be valid and helpful. Just be sure to pick and choose what is appropriate for your individual child and situation.

are the children who have them. Temper tantrums are not preplanned events. With rare exception, your child does not set out to willfully misbehave when he has a temper tantrum.

Temper Tantrums Lead to Delinquency

There is no evidence to prove this. Most of your child's temper tantrums are a result of developmental issues. If you help your child acquire self-control as she learns appropriate ways to express her strong emotions, you should expect her to become a happy and well-adjusted teen and adult.

You Are a Bad Parent Because Your Child Has Temper Tantrums

Wrong. There are many reasons why your child may have temper tantrums, and none of them is a reflection of your ability to parent. Even the children of child development experts have temper tantrums.

There Is Nothing You Can Do about Your Child's Tantrums

If that were true, this book would not exist. Although you have not caused your child's temper tantrums, there are many ways that you can prevent them. In addition, you can help your child to acquire the skills to express himself in a more appropriate fashion.

All Temper Tantrums Are for Manipulation

Wrong. This may be the most widely propagated myth. Many parenting books, and even well-meaning friends and family, will tell you to ignore your child when she has a temper tantrum. In fact, this is valid only for attention tantrums, which occur with minimal frequency in children older than three or four.

Responding to Your Child's Tantrum Spoils Him

Wrong. For many temper tantrum situations, the most appropriate response is to respond with compassion and gently guide your child. This is particularly true for the frustration and emotional temper tantrums that are common for toddlers. When young children are out of control, they need you to patiently help them reestablish emotional control.

You Should Always Have Full Control over Your Child

Wrong. Helping your child gain control over his actions does not mean that you must have full

Mindful Mommy

Recent surveys show that 68 percent of parents still approve of spanking as an appropriate discipline technique. But research shows that spanking a child has been tied to an increase in aggression and retaliation behaviors. Children who are spanked are more likely to lash out at other children who are aggressive toward them.

control over him. You should not try to break a child's spirit or will. Your ultimate goal is to help him become independent and able to regulate his own behavior, not depend on you to police his every move.

There Is One Right Way to Cope with Temper Tantrums

Wrong. Wrong. Wrong! Parenting is never a one-size-fits-all endeavor. There are many strategies for coping with your child's temper tantrums. What works for your child will be as unique as your child is. In fact, you are bound to discover that you need to be flexible, and as your child grows, you will need to adjust your response. You may even find that what worked last week does not work now. Flexibility is key.

Chapter 2

Your Child's Temperament, From Day One

DID YOU THINK YOU had parenting down to a fine art because raising your first child was a breeze? She was a happy-go-lucky and very calm baby? She was friendly and sunny and temper tantrums were few and far between. Now, your second child has come along and turned your understanding of parenting on its ear. You are sure you're doing exactly the same thing, but your second child seems so fussy and cranky all of the time. Even the slightest upsetting event will cause her to have a temper tantrum. Can it be true that some children are more prone to tantrums than others? Keep reading to find out!

Sunny? Cloudy? Disposition Explained

Some children are more prone to temper tantrums than other children are. Psychologists believe this may be due to a child's temperament. Temperament is your child's inborn disposition. Your child's temperament is his characteristic way of responding and reacting to events and his environment. Your child's temperament will be fairly stable throughout his life, but it is not set in stone. His temperament will surely be influenced by interactions and experience as he matures.

In the now classic New York Longitudinal Study, researchers identified nine basic temperamental traits. The variance of how a child exhibits these traits determines the child's temperament type as difficult, easy, slow to warm up, or mixed. Although most parents are unfamiliar with the nine identified traits by name, they know their child's temperament. In fact, more parents will observe these traits very early on. By the time a child is four months old, her temperament is usually apparent.

Breaking It Down: Three Common Temperaments

Psychologists have identified three main temperament types. It is important to note that each category

Mommy Knows Best

Don't be too quick to blame all your child's tantrums on her temperament! When questioning the cause of a temper tantrum, it is smart to ask yourself the following things before blaming temperament: Is the tantrum developmentally related (e.g., lack of language skills)? Is your child ill or under a lot of stress? Does your child have a developmental or behavioral disorder?

or type may encompass a wide range of behaviors. Very few children will be a perfect match to any one type of temperament. However, you may find that a majority of his behaviors fit in one of the three types listed below. Understanding these three main types will help you understand your own child better and, who knows, you might even recognize some of these traits in his friends, your older children, and yourself!

The Easy Child

You will be able to tell early on whether your child has an easy temperament. She will be a calm and content baby. Not much will seem to upset her. Her behavior is reasonably predictable. Not many things seem to startle or upset her. Loud noises, new people, strange places—she adjusts well and takes it all in stride.

Slow to Warm Up

If your child has a slow to warm up temperament, he will not be as easygoing as the child with an easy temperament is. Children with this temperament are often cautious about new people or situations, often withdrawing first and taking a while

Mommy Knows Best

As many as 35 percent of all children will not fit neatly into a type. Happily, close to 40 percent of all children can be classified as having an easy temperament. About 10 percent of children will have a slow to warm up temperament, and fewer than 15 percent will consistently display characteristics attributed to a difficult temperament.

before they feel comfortable. Additionally, it may take them longer to adjust to change.

Difficult

The child with a difficult temperament is often a feisty, cranky, or fussy baby. She reacts strongly to new people or situations. She seems to be upset easily, and it is difficult for her to calm down.

Traits Associated with the Three Types of Temperament

Trait	Easy	Difficult	Slow to Warm Up
Activity	low	high	low
Distract- ibility	low	high	moderate
Adaptability	good	poor	slow
Approach/ Withdrawal	approach	withdrawal	initial withdrawal
Intensity	low	high	mixed/low
Regularity/ Rhythm	regulated	unregulated	regulated
Sensory sensitivity	high	low	moderate
Mood	positive	negative	mixed
Persistence	low	high	moderate

Trait Him Well!

It will be helpful for you to know your child's temperament—or at least, to have an idea about it. By knowing this, you will gain valuable insight into your child and her behavior. If a child with a difficult temperament is challenging you, you probably wish to get at the root of the problem. Some parents report wondering if their child is emotionally disturbed or has brain damage. Perhaps you found yourself viewing your child in a negative light by labeling her as a crybaby or a wild child.

A child with a difficult temperament is as normal as a child with an easy or slow to warm up temperament. Once you know and understand your child's temperament, you can view your child's behavior objectively. This will help you to refrain from emotionally lashing out or withdrawing from your child. Understanding your child's temperament will give you the insight to plan accordingly and avoid potential problems for your child. For example, if you know your child is slow to adapt, you can be sure to warn him in advance before bedtime.

Traits Weakly Associated with Tantrums

These temperament traits are part of the nine that are considered when determining a child's temperament type. These traits do have a weaker relationship to tantrum behavior, but they are a part of your child's total temperament and affect his behavior and disposition.

Distractibility

If your child has a high level of distractibility, he will have a hard time paying attention. When he is engaged in a task, his attention is easily diverted by external stimuli such as background noises. It may seem that he has a hard time following directions, or that he is not listening to you at all. The child with a difficult temperament is more likely to have a high level of distractibility.

Activity Level

The child with a difficult temperament often has a high activity level. You will be able to observe this when your child is still an infant. The infant with a high activity level is restless, fidgety, and squirms a lot. As she grows, you will notice that she always seems to be on the go. She hates to be confined or constrained. Getting her into the car seat may be a battle every time. Additionally, you may find her so active that she becomes wild or out of control.

Persistence

Persistence is a mainly positive trait. A child who is usually able to attend well to a task without giving up is a persistent child. If your child is persistent, he is more likely to be able to tolerate frustration. There is a downside to having a child with a high level of persistence. At times, he may become stubborn in

Mindful Mommy

Some level of distractibility is normal for young children. The ability to focus comes with increased cognitive skills. Young children naturally have a short attention span. Sitting still for more than ten minutes can be quite a challenge for a young child.

his attempts at completing a task, even when it is not feasible. One mother relates, "My son refused to quit any task he started. If he was struggling to zip his jacket, he refused help. No matter that we may be running late; once he had a goal in mind, he would fight to accomplish it. If his dad or I stepped in, he would have a fit."

Regularity/Rhythm

This trait refers to the predictability of your child's patterns of sleep and hunger. Many infants will fall into a consistent sleep and hunger schedule at around four to eight weeks of age. If your child has low regularity, you will have difficulty getting her on a schedule. As she grows, bedtime conflicts may become common. Some nights you may find that she is cranky and falling asleep early, and other nights she may be wide awake, unable to settle down, and very resistant to bedtime.

Traits Strongly Associated with Tantrums

Some temperament traits are more strongly associated with temper tantrums. Here are traits commonly seen in children with difficult temperaments:

- Low adaptability
- Low sensory threshold
- Low approachability
- High intensity
- A negative mood

In many cases, you will be able to see a direct link between a trait and your child's troublesome behavior.

Adaptability

Many children with difficult temperaments have low adaptability. Adaptability is the ability to handle transition and change calmly. If your child has low adaptability, she becomes upset when there is a change in routine. She is unable to go with the flow. She may be very resistant to change. Anything unexpected easily throws her off balance.

Approach and Withdrawal

This trait refers to a child's response to new situations or people. Children with a difficult temperament are more likely to be cautious or anxious when meeting new people and may be clingy or shy in those circumstances. They are often resistant to trying new things, whether it is a new vegetable or a different brand of sneakers.

Mindful Mommy

Keep in mind that it's normal and fairly common for young children to experience some shyness. Even a child who is fairly outgoing may show some hesitation at first. The difference is, unlike a child with withdrawal, other children do not react strongly to all new situations, and their shyness will usually fade after ten to fifteen minutes.

Intensity

All children experience happiness and sadness. However, each child varies in the way he responds to his own emotions. For example, two children may win a prize at a carnival. One child smiles broadly and the other child jumps around shrieking and hollering. If your child has very intense reactions to emotion, he may have a more difficult temperament. The very intense child may react strongly to even the slightest displeasure, perhaps earning a reputation as a drama queen or king.

Sensory Threshold

Is your child very picky or fussy? She may have a low threshold for sensory stimulation if she responds strongly to mild stimulation from things such as noise, room temperature, pain, or odors. "Bath time was battle time," recalls one mom. "I could barely touch my daughter with the washcloth without her cringing. The water was always too hot or too cold. The soap was too slimy, and the shampoo stung her eyes. It was a nightmare."

Mood

This trait refers to the child's prevailing disposition. Even the most cheerful child will be in a bad mood on occasion. In contrast, the child with a negative mood trait seems chronically unhappy. He has a more pessimistic and negative outlook on life.

Parenting Style to Match Your Child

Although temperament is inborn, a child's experiences and environment do have an impact. There is a term that refers to a parenting approach that accounts for individual differences in your child's temperament—*goodness of fit*. Effective parenting is not one-size-fits-all. Your parenting style has goodness of fit when your expectations and demands match your child's temperament. Goodness of fit will help you respond appropriately to your child's unique temperamental traits.

It's important to be flexible and adjust your response to meet your child's temperament. You will find that there will be a higher probability for conflict if your own temperament varies greatly from your child's. If you are impatient, you may have a hard time holding back when your very persistent child insists on taking her time to complete a task. If you are outgoing in social situations, you may be displeased when your shy or withdrawn child does not approach your friends in a bold fashion.

Mommy Must

When your response to your child's temperament is not a good fit, you will have difficulty managing your child's temper tantrums. In addition, your child could experience stress if your expectations do not match his temperamental style.

Although much of goodness of fit relies on the way you respond to your child's specific temperamental traits, you can follow some basic guidelines:

- Do not try to change your child's temperament. Rather, show respect for your child's uniqueness.
- Avoid comparing your child to another child. Avoid statements like, "Why can't you sit still like your brother?" or "I never had a hard time spending the night away from home, and neither should you."
- Focus on the positive. Even traits associated with a difficult temperament can be positive. The intense child may also be creative. The slow to adapt child may be more analytical and methodical.

Tailor Your Response

Being sensitive to your child's individuality allows you to adapt your responses to calm your child rather than make things worse. You will eliminate a lot of stress and conflict with your child if you respond appropriately to his temperament traits. You will have a goodness of fit if your expectations and reactions match your child's temperament.

Working With a Slow-to-Adapt Child

If your child is slow to adapt, he thrives on predictability and routine. You will find that change and transition are difficult for him. You can prevent many problems if you establish a daily routine. Try to keep events in your child's life as predictable as possible.

Prepare your child in advance when there will be a change. This is helpful whether the change is small (lunch will be late) or large (she's starting a new school). Take time to discuss with your child what will be happening and what she can expect. If there is to be a major change in your child's life, maintain as many of your child's routines as possible. For example, while on vacation in a hotel, try to maintain your child's normal bedtime routine.

Every day of your child's life is filled with transitions: coming in from playing outside to get ready for dinner, taking a bath, and getting ready for bed. The slow to adapt child will have difficulty during these times. Often, your child will be deeply engaged in an activity and he will find it difficult to abruptly stop what he is doing. Give him a warning that he needs to end his activity soon. Be concrete and specific.

Mommy Knows Best

Probably the most difficult and common transition time for your child will be when you ask her to stop playing and clean up. This does not have to be a dreaded chore—you can make it fun. Try turning cleanup time into a game. Challenge your child to beat the clock. Perhaps you can pretend the toys are real and she is putting the dolls to bed, parking the cars, and so forth.

Rather than saying, "We are leaving soon," try telling him, "We will have to leave in five minutes, so you need to finish your project." Help him find closure by prompting, "What else do you wish to paint on the picture so that you feel it is finished?"

Learning to Be Comfortable

Many children are hesitant or cautious in new situations. They may be reluctant to enter a theme park, hesitant to go with you to visit the neighbors, or withdrawn when meeting new people. After ten to fifteen minutes though, most children become more comfortable in a new situation.

If your child is having great difficulty and withdraws or excessively resists new situations, there are some ways you can put him at ease.

Show appreciation. Everyone approaches new situations at his own speed. Let him know that this is okay.

Avoid labeling. Labeling her as shy has a negative connotation, and you may create a self-fulfilling prophecy.

Go slow. Encourage, but do not push your child to approach. Be sensitive to his level of comfort. If you push him, he is likely to feel anxious and he will resist more.

Avoid reinforcement. If you make a fuss and coddle your child when she is reserved, she may learn to increase the behavior for attention.

Stay quiet. Avoid speaking for your child. Speaking for him diminishes his need to approach people and speak for himself.

Make the challenge manageable. Break it into small steps. If your child is not ready to play the musical chairs game with the other children, perhaps she can help play the music for a while.

Recognize triumphs. Acknowledge when your child reaches out: "I am glad to see that you felt comfortable enough to say hello to Aunt Elise."

Dealing With Negativity

If your child has an overall negative mood and disposition, it is unlikely there is much you can do to change it. You can, however, help reduce her pessimism. Help her recognize the positive aspects of a situation. Take the time to point out the silver lining behind her gray cloud. For example, you could say, "Yes, the weather today is dreadful, but what a great day to pop some popcorn and watch a movie!" Encourage her to focus on the bright side by asking her questions like, "What was the funniest ride at the park?" or "What is something good that happened today?"

Entertain Your Active
and Energetic Child

There are two main strategies for coping with your highly active child. You can prevent problems, and you can give her appropriate outlets for her excess energy. Once you recognize this temperament trait in your child, you can anticipate situations that may be problematic for her.

Recognize that sitting still and waiting will be particularly trying. Places like doctor's offices and restaurants are likely to be unpleasant places to take your active child. If it is not possible to avoid these types of places, plan ahead to reduce potential problems. Take along a diversionary activity for your child, such as a handheld game. While you are there, scout out opportunities for your child to get up and move around. Choose restaurants with play areas or at least a buffet with plenty of room. When you are in a waiting room, sometimes even a brief walk up the corridor can be helpful.

Give your active child plenty of opportunities to burn off steam. Whenever possible, balance quiet activities with more active ones. One smart father found a way to make long car trips with his son manageable. He took the time to pull off the road for a break every hour. They got out of the car and did exercises such as running in place or jumping jacks. This father found that the time lost for these "pit stops" paid off with a calmer, more pleasant trip for everyone.

Focus! Focus!

It can be very frustrating if you feel that your child is never paying attention to you. When your child does listen, she often only completes half a task before wandering off, mentally, if not physically.

Multi-step tasks are particularly difficult, as your child may become distracted midway through completing the task. Keep directions simple and break them down step by step. Instead of saying, "Go over to your dresser, get your blue socks out of the top drawer, fold them, and put them in your suitcase," try, "Go to your dresser. Okay—now that you are there, open your top drawer." Alternatively, you may find it helpful to prompt your child to keep him on task when he seems to get lost with multi-step tasks: "Okay, you folded the socks, now where should you put them?"

Is Your Child Overreacting?

Children with difficult temperaments often respond to situations with a high level of intensity. Whereas a cut on the finger may cause one child to whine and ask for a Band-Aid, the intense child may scream as if she has been mortally wounded.

Mommy Must

Make an effort to capture and hold your child's attention. Approach your child directly, rather than calling out from the other room. Use his name when speaking to him. Whenever possible, get down to his level and make eye contact.

It is a natural response to mirror someone's behavior and emotions. In other words, when someone is whispering, you will be inclined to whisper, too. This is especially true when your angry child is screaming and crying. You may find that your automatic response is to yell and exhibit anger as well. This behavior will usually cause your child's intensity to escalate, so it is important that you stay calm.

A child with a high level of intensity will be the most inclined to lose emotional control. It will be helpful if you tune in to your child. Learn to recognize her signals that indicate a flare-up is approaching. This is the best time to intervene. Help your child become self-aware, too, as you attempt to squelch her outburst prematurely. "I can see that the puzzle is really starting to frustrate you. Why don't we go for a walk, and then we can work on the puzzle later, when you feel calm."

Chapter 3

Cope with Care and Confidence

EVERY CHILD IS DIFFERENT and so is each tantrum! In fact each temper tantrums you witness is likely to be as unique as your child is. As she grows, why and how she throws temper tantrums are sure to change. You will find that how you respond to them may change depending on her age and development. However, you will find that there are some helpful general guidelines for responding to and guiding your child. So be adaptable and attentive—the most important thing is to help your child get through this tough time.

Regulate Your Emotional Response

When your child is in the throes of a temper tantrum and she is kicking and screaming, you are likely to have an emotional reaction. It is helpful to remember that many, if not all, parents have a hard time coping with their child's temper tantrums from time to time. You may experience any of the following emotions when your child is having a temper tantrum:

- embarrassment
- aggravation
- helplessness
- guilt
- anger

All of these feelings are normal. It is also normal to doubt your own parenting ability at times like these. When your child is having frequent emotional meltdowns, you may be asking, "Am I spoiling her too much? Why can't I prevent this?"

How Do You Feel? Watch Your Response!

How you feel when your child has a temper tantrum is likely to vary each time. Sometimes, you may find yourself very agitated with your child's behavior and other times you may feel calm and patient. Your feelings and responses will be influenced by how you perceive your child's motivation for his behavior. If you assume your child's motivation is negative (spite or attention), you will be more likely to feel angry or agitated. Consider, do you automatically think the worst? You may be able to change how you feel and subsequently respond. Avoid blame, and focus on the facts. Rather than attributing motivation to the behavior ("She is trying to push my buttons"), think about what is actually taking place ("She is crying when I tell her to put away her toys").

Your Child Might Mirror Your Anger!

Most parents occasionally report feeling angry when their child has a temper tantrum. If you respond to your child with anger or extreme emotion, you are likely to only fuel the fire. Your child's emotional response will often mirror your own. If you begin yelling or crying, you cannot effectively help to calm your child. Someone in the situation needs to be in control.

Examine your emotional response to your child's temper tantrums. You may be able to identify what triggers your impatience or anger. If there are specific situations that are trying for you, maybe you can find a way to avoid them. For example, bath time always becomes battle time. You are tired from a long day at work, and you just want to get your child into bed so you can relax. Perhaps you can ask your spouse to take over bath time, or you can move bath time to an earlier time in the evening when you are not so tired.

Mommy Must

When your child is in the throes of a temper tantrum, he may verbally lash out at you. Hearing your child announce, "I hate you!" may hurt you or anger you. Resist the temptation to respond emotionally. Recognize that your child is emotionally out of control, and he does not mean what he is saying.

There still may be times when you will feel angry that your child is having a temper tantrum. Take a deep breath. Try the well-known technique of slowly counting to ten. If you are still too angry or upset, take a step back from the situation. You can set a good example for your child on how to manage anger. Say something like, "I am feeling very angry about your behavior. I need to sit down and calm myself." If your child is very young or is in danger of hurting himself, be sure that another adult can step in while you step back from the situation.

Stick to a Style that Works for You Both

There are many reasons why your child has temper tantrums. Some of those reasons are internal factors such as your child's temperament, his verbal ability, his cognitive maturity, or even his level of hunger or fatigue. Some reasons are external situations, including stress, loud noises, separation, and loss. Very rarely will you personally be the direct cause of your child's tantrum. However, the way that you respond to your child's misbehavior and temper tantrums can either reduce or increase the likelihood of problems.

Psychologist Diana Baumrind has identified three basic parenting styles. Each style looks at the balance of control in the parent–child relationship and its influence on the child's behavior and development. It is important to note that you will probably not fit exclusively into one category. Although you may find most of your responses fitting into one category, your parenting style may vary. Your mood, the circumstances, and even the birth order of your child may influence your parenting style.

To find out what your parenting style is, choose the answer that best describes your response or view:

1. Your child starts to whine and cry because he doesn't want to take a bath. You:
   (a) Give up, and try again tomorrow.
   (b) Ignore your child's protest. You will remove his clothes yourself if you have to.
   (c) Question him on why he is upset and then find a way to reassure him.

2. Your child asks to stay up late to watch a special TV show. You say:
   (a) "That is up to you, if you think you won't be tired in the morning."
   (b) "Absolutely not! Your bedtime is always at 8:00, you know that."
   (c) "Why don't you tell me why the show is worth staying up for and I will consider it."

Mommy Knows Best

Studies show that there are some specific parenting practices that are associated with more aggressive behavior in children. Some of these practices include: poor supervision, a low involvement in the child's interests and activities, and harsh or erratic discipline.

3. When it comes to setting limits for your child, you generally believe:
   (a) Children should learn to set their own rules. Freedom will help them learn.
   (b) Your rules are the law. What you say goes.
   (c) Rules are important guidelines for behavior, but there may be exceptions.

4. Your child forgot to feed his goldfish again. You:
   (a) Feed the goldfish.
   (b) Punish your child by finding a new home for the goldfish.
   (c) Ask your child what will help him remember to feed the goldfish. Perhaps a sticky note on his door?

5. Your child is refusing to sleep in her own bed. You:
   (a) Let her sleep where she wants.
   (b) Admonish her for not being in bed after her bedtime.
   (c) Talk to her about things that might make her feel more comfortable sleeping in her own bed.

Permissive parents will answer mainly A.
Authoritarian parents choose answer B the most.
Authoritative parents are most inclined to select C.

What are these types?

Is Your Style Permissive?

The permissive parent gives most of the control to the child. She fails to set reasonable limits and often does not consistently enforce the limits that she has established. Permissive parents often allow the child to make decisions, and they count on their children to regulate their own behavior. Children of permissive parents are often uncertain or anxious about whether they are behaving appropriately. They are less likely to take risks or try new things. Additionally, children of permissive parents tend to develop less self-control.

Is Your Style Authoritarian?

Authoritarian parents insist that they have full control. They expect their child to behave with unquestioning obedience. The children of authoritarian parents do not have a voice, and they make very few choices. The child is expected to fully conform and comply with all expectations without question. These children are more prone to temper tantrums. They are also more likely to be more withdrawn and distrustful than other children are.

Mindful Mommy

There are many factors that will influence your style and approach to parenting. How you were raised will play a part, as well as whether you choose to reject or follow the style your parents used. Your own temperament, values, and beliefs about how children should behave will also impact your style.

Children of authoritarian parents are also the most likely to exhibit rebellious behavior when they get older.

Is Your Style Authoritative?

Authoritative parents share control with their children. Although they remain the authority, they encourage and respect their child's opinions and input. The child's voice is heard and her preferences are taken into account during decision making. Authoritative parents set consistent, reasonable, and firm standards of behavior. The child with authoritative parents is the most likely to be secure and self-reliant and to exhibit the most self-control.

What's Age Got to Do With It?

Temper tantrums are a normal part of your child's development. As your child grows, you will find that your child will have temper tantrums for different reasons. Additionally, there are different guidelines and strategies for each age group.

Toddlers

Toddlerhood is the peak time for temper tantrums. Common causes for toddler temper tantrums include: separation anxiety, an inability to understand another's point of view, a desire for autonomy, and immature verbal skills. Almost all toddler tantrums are the result of developmental issues. Toddlers do not intentionally engage in tantrum behavior for revenge or to get attention. They are socially, emotionally, and intellectually incapable of that thought process.

With gentle guidance, allow your toddler's temper tantrum to run its course. You will be better equipped for coping with a tantrum if you recognize that! Your young child needs an avenue for expressing and venting frustration, anger, and other strong emotions. Do not view your acceptance of your child's temper tantrums as being permissive. You are not coddling or spoiling her. Just be sure that you are not rewarding her with extra attention or praise for having a tantrum. The message you want to convey is, "I understand that you have strong feelings to work out. I am going to help you find more appropriate ways to express those feelings."

Your young toddler has not yet developed emotional control. Therefore, he may be frightened and overwhelmed by both his strong feelings and his loss of control. Many toddlers can be calmed down by being held. This may help them feel a sense of security and external control. Each child is different,

Mommy Must

Because they tend to lose both physical and emotional control, toddlers are the most likely to injure themselves during a tantrum. You need to stay calm and keep close to your toddler during a temper tantrum. You may even find that you will need to manage her safety by moving things out of her way, or holding her securely.

though. Some distraught toddlers will find that being held is too restrictive and agitating.

Your toddler has a short attention span. You may be able to diffuse many of her temper tantrums by simply distracting her or redirecting her attention. When she is yelling for a candy bar at the store, you may be able to get away with a diversionary tactic like, "Look! I wonder what those balloons are for. Let's go see!" (Of course, this particular tactic is only okay if it is all right for your toddler to have a balloon.) When she is insisting on cutting her baby doll's hair, you might be able to redirect her interest to cutting paper scraps instead.

Preschoolers

Your preschooler should be having fewer temper tantrums than he did as a toddler. Common causes of tantrums for preschoolers include difficulty sharing, impatience, and frustration. Although many of your preschooler's temper tantrums may be caused by immaturity, you may now begin to see your child use tantrum behavior as a form of manipulation to get what he wants or to get attention.

Your preschooler has many skills that can help her manage and express her emotions without having temper tantrums. You may simply need to guide her to use these skills. She is now less egocentric. She is learning how to see someone else's perspective, and she is developing empathy. When she is having a conflict with another child, you can simply ask her, "How do you think Carly feels when you push her?" If she is not able to answer this question, or is not yet ready to empathize, model by answering how you would feel in this situation. Be sure to capitalize on her improved verbal skills; encourage her to use words when she is angry or upset.

Older Children

Older children are typically more tolerant of frustration, and they have developed some self-control. You may still see your older child have an occasional temper tantrum. Although he has new abilities, he also faces new challenges. Some common causes for temper tantrums in your older child may include: difficulty in delaying gratification, frustration in tackling new physical skills or academic challenges, social rejection, and a desire for independence.

Your older child is more rational and logical. You should be able to reason and negotiate with him. Your focus here is not to control or manage your child's behavior. Instead, you need to help him develop the skills he needs to manage his own emotions and behavior. You can help your child to cope with his strong emotions as well as develop self-calming techniques and problem-solving skills. Chapter 18 will show you how to teach your child these skills.

Understand Internal Factors

Why is your child having so many temper tantrums? Sure, you may be looking at their temperament or possible the influence of recent stressful events in the household. However, the solution to preventing many of your child's temper tantrums may be even closer. Learn how internal factors such as hunger, fatigue, and sensory stimulation can effect your child's behavior.

A Hungry Child is a Cranky Child

Proper nutrition is crucial for your child's growth and health. What and when your child eats will effect their physical well-being as well as their behavior. Just like adults, hungry children are more likely to be irritable, aggressive and easily upset.

The best way for you to prevent your child from being hungry and experiencing mid-day slumps and irritability is to provide your child with small and frequent meals. Rather than serving your child three traditional meals each day, divide the daily portions into five or six mini meals or snacks. While your child is awake, attempt to have something to eat available for them every three or four hours.

The Influence of Sleep Deprivation

Sleep is a biological need, essential for survival. Not only does sleep give the body a chance to rest and heal, but it is necessary for healthy brain functioning as well. A good night's sleep regenerates and rejuvenates us, getting us ready to face the challenges of a new day with a fresh perspective.

Young children, in particular, need regular and adequate sleep to maintain both their physical and emotional health. There is a long list of behaviors associated with inadequate sleep, including:

- decreased concentration
- diminished attention span
- increased irritability and restlessness
- lowered energy and activity levels
- problems with coordination
- defensiveness
- anxiety
- increased impatience

It is easy to see how many of these behaviors can be associated with an increased tendency for temper tantrums. Research shows that when preschoolers get less than the recommended amount of sleep in a twenty four-hour period, the children were 25% more likely to display opposition, noncompliance, or aggressive behavior.

Sensory Overload

How your child responds and reacts to their physical environment and external stimuli can influence their behavior. Almost all children will have some sensitivity to sensory stimulation that can result in behavioral problems.

Some children will exhibit the temperament trait of low sensory threshold discussed in chapter 2. These children will be over-reactive to smells, sights and /or sounds. They may respond as if they are literally being bombarded by too much stimulation.

You will sometimes witness them avoiding and withdrawing by observable behaviors such as holding their ears or closing their eyes when they are overwhelmed.

Determine Tantrum Triggers

The more you understand your child's temper tantrums, the better equipped you will be to cope with them. If you are able to identify what triggers a tantrum, you will have a better chance of preventing it. Keep track of your child's temper tantrums over a period of time—two or three weeks should be sufficient. It is wise to include input from any adults who interact with your child. They may be able to provide a fresh perspective. Be sure to include details on what happens so you will be able to recall the incident clearly.

It is worthwhile to keep a written diary or journal. A written journal will help you reflect back on your child's behavior. You will be able to look for patterns so that you can avoid conditions and situations that you discover are problematic. A written journal will also help you to be realistic and objective. Keep track of when tantrums happen, where, who is around, signs that led up to the tantrum, how your child reacted, and what it took to calm him down. Take a look at this sample journal entry for some help.

Variable	Comments
Day of week	Tuesday
Time of day	Late afternoon
Who	It was just me
Warning signs	He was whining for a cookie about 20 minutes earlier.
Place	In front of the shoe store
What happened	He suddenly threw himself on the ground. Through his sobs, I heard him say, "No, I don't wanna go to the store."
Conclusion	I moved him over to a bench. I told him that I needed him to use words so I could help him. Finally, he was able to tell me he was hungry.
Comments	I think maybe hunger and fatigue got the best of him today.

After you've tracked her tantrums for a few days or weeks, look closely at the entries to try to discern a pattern. Are your child's temper tantrums occurring more often on certain days? If so, can you identify why that day may be problematic? Perhaps Mondays are particularly hectic, or Friday is the day when Aunt Sue comes to visit.

Are your child's temper tantrums occurring more at a certain time of the day? Maybe you will discover that your child is prone to temper tantrums when she is cranky in the morning, or right before dinner when she is getting hungry.

Who was present when your child had a temper tantrum? Do certain people seem to agitate your child? Is your child more likely to experience a separation tantrum with you? Is he more prone to stage a tantrum for attention when he is visiting Grandma?

Did your child exhibit any warning signs that he was about to lose control? If you can pinpoint the precursors to your child's temper tantrum, you may be able to begin intervening before things get out of hand. Early signs that your child is heading toward a tantrum may include one or many of the following: irritability, increased crankiness, sudden resistance to physical affection, and whining.

Is your child showing a tendency to have more tantrums in certain places? You may find that certain places are too stressful or stimulating for your child, and you may wish to avoid those places for a while.

Communicate Positively

When you respond to your child's temper tantrums, what you say can have a big impact. When you talk to your child, you have the opportunity to calm her down and help her learn safe behavior and good self-control. Positive communication will promote these

Mommy Knows Best

You may also wish to record how your child's temper tantrum was resolved. Was your child able to regain control independently? How did you respond to his behavior? Reviewing this information from a selected period of time may help you gain a better understanding of what is effective and what is not for coping with your child's tantrums.

goals. Additionally, when you use positive communication, you can boost her self-esteem and confidence. When you use positive communication to respond to your child's temper tantrums, you are focusing on the behavior, not the child. You are saying, "I accept you, but I do not accept your behavior."

Positive Statements

Your goal is to help your child learn safe behavior and self-control. It is important that you are clear when stating your expectations of your child's behavior. Most young children are given negative directions such as, "Stop that!" or "Don't do that!" When you tell your child, "Don't throw sand," there is no guidance or direction given. What should the child do? By changing your response to, "Keep the sand in the sandbox," you change the focus from a correction of her behavior to an instruction about what she should do. Your child may be readily able to conform to your expected behavior, and he will be more likely to do so independently. When you use the positive statement technique, "Don't run over there" becomes "Please walk on the sidewalk." "Stop coloring on the walls" becomes "Use your crayons for coloring only on paper."

"I" messages

"I" messages are automatically positive statements that state or define your expectations. They are usually met with less defensiveness and resistance and can be a powerful tool in communication. Notice the difference in tone between these two sentences:

- "Why are you such a slob? Can't you ever clean your room?"
- "I would like for you to pick up the toys and clothes off the floor."

Which of these is more likely to result in your child's compliance? Effective "I" messages can start with "I need," "I want," "I wish," and so forth. When you are using an "I" message, "You are too loud" becomes "I need for you to use an indoor voice." "It is mean to tease the cat" becomes "I want you to pet the cat gently."

Reflective Listening

Reflective listening is particularly helpful with children who are experiencing strong feelings, and for children who cannot have their desires met. The reflective listening technique has two parts. In the first part of the statement, you reflect or rephrase what you see or hear in your child's behavior. Like a mirror, you reflect her feelings back to her. The

Mindful Mommy

"I" messages can be a very effective way to establish positive communication with anyone of any age. Encourage your child to also use this technique. When your child uses an "I" message, he is intentionally and clearly stating his needs. This is a big improvement from when he used tantrum behaviors to communicate.

second part is your statement of contradiction or reality. For example, "I can see you are very angry right now, but I need you to put the blocks away," or "I know you want to see over the fence, but it is not safe for you to stand up there."

Avoid These Reactions

Your positive responses can help your child calm down and cope with temper tantrums. However, negative responses and statements will ultimately sabotage your efforts. It is easy to fall into a pattern of using these responses. These negative responses are ones to avoid, as they will often lower your child's self esteem, confidence, and trust, which are needed for your child to develop self-control.

Threats, Warnings, and Consequences

You may have threatened your child, "If you do not settle down, I am going to leave you here." There is a difference between warnings and threats. When you warn your child, you are stating the certain consequences to his behavior. Try saying something like, "If you don't settle down, we are going to go outside until you regain control." By contrast, when you threaten your child, you are mentioning a consequence you have no intention of using. These stated consequences are usually exaggerated and intended to intimidate or frighten your child; they often include abandonment, imprisonment, and physical harm. If you often threaten your child without following through, your child will quickly learn to disregard both your threats and warnings.

Guilt-Tripping Your Child

"I am going to have to miss my meeting because you are acting up." When you attempt to blame your child or make her feel ashamed, you are using guilt. If you make your child feel guilty, she is likely to doubt her own competence and worth. She may feel that she will never measure up. Children who feel guilty are usually less autonomous and confident. Additionally, your child may also begin using blame to account for his own behavior. When your child blames others for his behavior, he fails to take personal responsibility for his own actions and choices.

Don't Join the Name Calling Game!

"Stop screaming! You are such a brat!" Calling your child "lazy," "evil," "stupid," "sloppy," or "wild" is not an effective way to respond to her behavior. She will take these labels to heart. This often leads to a self-fulfilling prophecy, where she internalizes

Mindful Mommy

Some guilt-inducing statements inadvertently give power to your child. When you say, "Now look what you have made me do!" or "It is your fault that I scream so much," you are telling your child that she has the ability to affect your mood or behavior. Avoid this, or your child may begin manipulating you.

and meets those negative expectations. For example, a child that hears that he is lazy will be more likely to be lazy.

Comparisons Aren't Fair

"Why can't you behave like your sister Anna does?" When you compare one child with another, you sow the seeds of resentment and bitterness between them. Again, comparisons can also damage your child's self-esteem. The only appropriate way to compare is if you compare your child with herself, by noticing how she has changed or grown. For example, "Wow, your manners have really improved since the last time we went to eat at a restaurant."

Chapter 4

The Rules of Response

KNOWING HOW TO RESPOND to your child when he is having a tantrum is a serious challenge! It can be very frustrating—you don't need to be told this! And every mom wants a tantrum to end as quickly as it came on. So how can you get your child to calm down? Consider this: the root of a temper tantrum is the loss of self-control. When your child is young, you have the ability to help him learn self-control and safe, appropriate behavior. How you respond to misbehavior, whether you choose to use punishment, rewards, or discipline techniques, will influence your child's ability to maintain self-control later on.

You Can Shape Your Child's Behavior

Every behavior has a result. At a very young age, children begin learning how their behavior leads to a result. When they toss their spoon on the floor, it makes a noise. When they cry, Mom comes and comforts them. These results (also called consequences or reinforcement) can be either positive or negative.

A positive consequence to a behavior increases the likelihood that your child will repeat the behavior in the hope of achieving the desired result. For example, if you praise your child for sitting still at the movie, she will be more likely to sit still the next time—because she wants to receive the praise. Conversely, a negative result will increase the likelihood that your child will stop a behavior to avoid the negative consequence. If you take away a favorite toy when she does not put it in her toy box, she will be more likely to pick up the other toys to avoid losing any more. By choosing your response carefully, you can shape your child's behavior.

Studies show that positive consequences are more motivating and influential on behavior than negative consequences are. Children will be more motivated to do something for a reward than they will be to avoid a punishment. It is worthwhile to use positive consequences when your child is behaving in a desirable manner. And you should avoid responding with positive consequences if your child is misbehaving. This seems logical but you may find you are doing

Mommy Must

Because young children are just learning the principles of cause and effect, and their memory is not long, consequences need to occur soon after the behavior. The famous threat "just wait until we get home" has little impact on a young child, who will not associate a later punishment with his behavior four hours earlier at the mall.

just that. Suppose your child is interrupting you while you are on the telephone, so you give her a cookie to occupy her. Your child is having a tantrum and kicking the seat in front of him at the movies, so you put him on your lap. Remember that some children may sometimes view even negative attention (lecturing, yelling) as a positive consequence. This is particularly true for children who feel like negative attention is better than no attention. Consider carefully what is reinforcing to your child before you respond.

Many children learn to engage in some behaviors just for the attention or reaction it brings. These behaviors include whining, tattling, and swearing. Imagine a young child who uses a swear word without understanding its meaning. He sees his parents react with shock, receives a lecture, and quickly learns that he can bring a halt to adult conversation and divert attention to himself by using this word. Quite a lot of power for a child! But if parents instead react calmly to the child's use of a swear word, it doesn't create the same reinforcement. Say to your child, "That word hurts people's feelings. If you wish to speak with me, use polite words." Then ignore further swearing. Your child has no incentive to use the word to get attention, because you don't make a fuss.

Should You Praise Your Little One?

One type of positive reinforcement you may choose to use to shape your child's behavior is praise. You can help your child understand your expectations and then have her conform to them. When you praise your child, you recognize the times your child behaves the way you wish, and you are encouraging her to continue to repeat the behavior.

Praise can be very reinforcing and motivational to your child. Praise may also help boost your child's self-esteem. Praise communicates your approval and acceptance of her behavior. The more she is concerned with your opinion, the more your praise will influence her behavior.

However, you must use praise sparingly. Your child's self-image can become closely tied to your praise. If he comes to expect it frequently, he may be hurt when you do not praise him. Some children can become dependent on praise and dependent on someone's evaluating their every move. Just like flattery, praise loses its impact when it is overused. Your child will probably not attach much value to your recognition of a major accomplishment if he's used to hearing lavish praise all the time. For example, "Wow, look how nice you are sitting at the table. Great job using your fork. Oh my! I am so proud of you for eating a carrot!" Your child will not be as

Mommy Knows Best

Do not forget that there are other positive ways to acknowledge your child's efforts or accomplishments. Sometimes simple gestures will do the trick. Try these: a wink, a high five, a broad smile, a hug, or a pat on the back.

motivated when you say, "You did a wonderful job writing your English essay."

When Is Praise Most Effective?

Praise is most effective if you make it clear which behavior you are acknowledging. You are showing approval of the child's behavior, not their character. You may also choose to praise specific accomplishments or effort. Praise phrases such as "Way to go" or "Good job" are often not specific enough to influence your child's behavior and encourage him to repeat the desired behavior. Here are some examples of specific and clear praise:

- "I am glad that you remembered to say 'please.'"
- "Good work in waiting for your turn."
- "I really like how you shared your blocks with your sister."
- "Super! I am pleased that you helped Mom with the dishes."
- "You worked so hard on your science project, and it shows."

Rewarding Results

In the long run, positive discipline techniques will be the most effective in helping your child learn safe behavior or self-control. There may be times, though, that you wish to react or respond immediately to a specific behavior or habit that your child has adopted.

When your child is exhibiting a behavior you do not like and wish to discourage, your first step is to identify and address the cause or issue. Don't forget, many temper tantrums are caused by specific triggers you can reduce! When your child is in control and making a clear choice with her behavior, you may wish to try a token or treat system of reinforcement. Treats and tokens work best if your child is older than five years old. Younger children have a hard time delaying gratification. Each time your child behaves as you wish or completes a specified task, you reward him with a token (poker chip, coin) or a mark (check mark, sticker) on a visual chart. He is then able to redeem the token or marks for a prize. These systems can be particularly effective for children because they are concrete and visual ways to measure or track success.

Set Up a System

Keep things simple. Be very specific regarding what behavior you are targeting. Avoid vague goals like "behave in the store" or "play nice." Rather, clearly define specific behavioral expectations: "Stay seated in the cart" or "Share your toy with your friend." Define exactly what she needs to do, when she needs to do it, and how well she needs to do it. For example, "Every time that we go to the grocery store, you must stay seated in the cart's seat. You must keep your bottom on the seat and not stand up until I remove you."

What Type of Reward?

If you use tokens, what item will you use? How will they be collected or stored? For charts, will you use check marks, stars? Will you recognize different levels of compliance? For example, you may choose to have blue chips if your child completed the task independently. Red chips may be used if you had to remind him once. You could use white chips if you had to ask him directly more than once. For younger children though, it is best to keep it simple and just have just one level.

When can he redeem his rewards for a prize? Every day? Once a week? You may wish to have small and larger prizes available. This way, he can choose to redeem one or two chips/stickers at the end of the day for a small prize or save some to earn a larger reward at the end of the week.

You do not have to be extravagant. Simple tokens or prizes often work well. Be sure to choose something that is age appropriate and of interest to your child. Here are some possible rewards:

- Mini deck of cards
- Super ball

Mommy Must

Limit the period of the reward system. As soon as your child begins to master the behavior consistently, you need to phase out the program so she does not rely solely on the reward. This usually happens in three or four weeks.

- Coloring book
- Pack of gum
- Hair ribbons
- Trading cards
- Puzzle book
- Mini action figures
- Stickers
- Spinning top
- Silly sunglasses

Don't Shower that Child with Gifts!

You may choose to give a chip/sticker each time the child behaves as you wish. You may also wish to reward after a set time. For example, "If you say 'please' at least once today, at bedtime I will put a star on the chart." Remember, the younger your child, the sooner he needs recognition or reinforcement. After your child starts to comply on a consistent basis, you may wish to stagger the reinforcement schedule. Instead of giving your child a sticker every time he shares a toy, give him a sticker every third time he shares a toy. After another few days, you can increase the interval time until your child is no longer expecting or depending on the reward to be motivated.

Mommy Knows Best

Avoid using food as a reward. Experts agree that using food as a reward or punishment sends the wrong messages. From this practice, unhealthy attitudes and habits about food could emerge.

You may choose to put priority on which behaviors you will reward. After all, it is not practical to reward every good deed and kind word. Alternatively, you may taper off the frequency with which you use rewards. As you do this, you can focus your child's attention on possible intrinsic rewards: "Look how happy you made Tony feel. Doesn't it feel good to help out a friend?"

Use rewards sparingly. If you rely on them constantly, your child will come to expect them. Eventually your child will be behaving as you wish because she is motivated by the reward. Her intrinsic (internal) motivation will diminish. She won't behave appropriately for self-motivating reasons such as self-worth or altruism. If this happens, once the rewards stop, so will the desired behavior. No longer will she cheerfully volunteer to help you carry groceries or help her little sister with homework because she enjoys being helpful and kind. Each time she behaves positively, she will be wondering, "What is in it for me?"

Punishment and Discipline: Two Different Things!

If you are like most parents, you view discipline and punishment as interchangeable approaches to guiding your child's behavior. In fact, they are very different. Each one has a unique set of goals, techniques, and outcomes. Often your role in discipline is that of a teacher guiding your child and teaching him safe behavior and self-control. When you punish your child, your role is more likely like that of a police officer.

Because it directly teaches appropriate behavior and teaches skills, discipline is more effective than punishment for handling your child's unwanted behavior. Additionally, recognizing and reinforcing positive behavior is more influential in changing your child's behavior. Besides having differing goals and strategies, punishment and discipline affect the child in different ways. Punishment often humiliates, degrades, angers, embarrasses, or discourages. Discipline often builds self-esteem, shows respect, models coping skills, and encourages.

Defining Discipline as Proactive

Discipline is largely a positive, proactive approach. The main goal of discipline is for your child to learn safe behavior and self-control. Ultimately, discipline helps your child to regulate her own behavior so that she is able to make independent choices and decisions. Positive discipline can teach children many things, such as:

- How to delay gratification
- How to develop a system of values and morals to guide them
- How to behave appropriately in a variety of settings

- How to follow societal and cultural standards of behavior
- How to use conflict resolution when relating with other people
- How to predict consequences of their behavior

The techniques discussed here will help your child to go beyond behaving just for a reward or praise or to avoid punishment. These strategies will help him develop an intrinsic motivation and inner control for behaving appropriately.

Which Direction? Redirection

Redirection is a powerful discipline technique for younger children. You guide the child to change his behavior to be safer and/or more appropriate. When you witness your child misbehaving, help him change either the action or the victim (person or object). Let's look at some ways that you can practice redirection:

Original Behavior	Change of Action	Change of Target
Cutting doll's hair	Brush doll's hair	Cut paper
Coloring on the table	Wipe table	Color on paper
Feeding Play-Doh to pet fish	Feed fish food to fish	Feed Play-Doh to pretend fish

Redirection works best when you guide the child gently, explaining why the change is needed. For example, "Jumping on the bed is not safe. If you feel like jumping, let's go outside and do jumping jacks" or "Jumping on the bed is not safe. Beds are for resting, so if you want to be on the bed, you need to lie down."

There Will Be Consequences!

You will not always be there to guide your child's actions. She needs to learn the consequences of her behavior. If you use consequences, you will help your child learn to think before acting and will teach her to take responsibility for her decisions. The main message to this technique is "Let the result fit the action." There are a couple of different types of consequences, let's take a look:

Natural consequences are also known as life experiences or "the school of hard knocks." You do not choose a response to your child's behavior; there is a natural result: If she skips breakfast, she will be hungry later. If she breaks a toy, she will no longer have that toy to play with. There are times when it is not appropriate to allow your child to experience natural consequences. If the consequences are in any way harmful for your child (such as drinking a poisonous chemical or cutting himself with a knife), you must stop the behavior and use a different discipline technique, such as redirection.

Logical consequences occur when your response imitates real life. If your child colors on the wall, then he must help wipe it off. If your teen does not put his socks in the laundry, then he will have to wash the socks himself or wear dirty socks. It is helpful that you impose logical consequences that ask for your child to repair or "make good" on his misbehavior.

Time-out

Time-out is a technique that has gained popularity recently. It can be an effective tool, but it is often overused. It is best not to use time-out for offenses when redirection or even a simple discussion will do. Reserve the technique as a time and place for the child to step back and get control. When your child is hurting others, a time-out may be necessary to separate her from the other children so she can regain control.

Be sure to explain to your child why you are putting her into time-out. You may say something like, "You are out of control and could hurt the baby. I am going to have you come away from him and sit in time-out. You need to calm down so you can

Mindful Mommy

Your young child's attention span is very short. For time-out to be effective, it should occur right when you intervene, as soon as the child misbehaves. Most experts recommend that you limit the time your child spends in time-out to one minute for every year of his age. So, for example, a four-year-old would spend a maximum of four minutes in time-out.

play safely." Choose an area for time-out that is easy for you to supervise. Also, try to have time-out in a location that is not overstimulating or rewarding. It is common for parent's to say "go to your room," but beware of this tactic. If you think about it, you may not want to use the child's bedroom. She may start to view this as a negative place and be reluctant to go there when you wish her to, such as at bedtime.

Punishment Proves Reactive

The main goal of punishment is to stop a child from misbehaving at the moment. Most parents also punish their child in the hopes that they will deter the child from repeating the behavior. Whereas discipline is often proactive, punishment is often simply reactive. You react to the child as you see her misbehave.

Types of Punishment

There are three main types of punishment: consequential punishments, verbal punishments, and physical punishments. Consequential punishment is different from the positive discipline techniques

Mommy Must

If you yell and carry on when your child is having a temper tantrum, you may unintentionally be giving him what he wanted, and therefore he will repeat the behavior. This is particularly true for children who are craving attention. To them, negative attention is better than no attention at all. Don't fall for this!

of logical and natural consequences. When a child misbehaves, there are still direct results of a behavior that occur, but unlike the discipline techniques, consequential punishment does not directly relate to the behavior. When you use a consequential punishment, you remove privileges or possessions that are valuable to your child. For example, "If you do not stop screaming at your sister, you can't go to the zoo" or "No TV if you don't clean your room." It is important to note that younger children truly have a hard time understanding the cause-and-effect relationship. Even older children often view this punishment as unfair or arbitrary, and it rarely produces long-term results.

Verbal punishment includes threatening, yelling, belittling, or embarrassing.

Keep in mind that calmly explaining the reasons for a rule and discussing possible solutions for misbehavior is not punishment. Lastly, physical punishment is rarely effective and includes spanking, pinching, slapping, and shaking.

To Spank or Not to Spank?

Spanking is a physical form of punishment. It is not a type of discipline, as it does not teach safe behavior or self-control. It sends a message that hitting is an appropriate way to respond when you are displeased or angry with someone.

Spanking your child when he is being aggressive is about as logical as screaming at him when he forgets to use a quiet voice. Spanking a child sends a mixed message: "Hitting is not acceptable unless you are bigger or angry." Children who are spanked, even infrequently, are more likely to become angry and then even more aggressive. They may show this anger in retaliation against you. Additionally, they may displace their anger toward an innocent target such as a younger sibling or perhaps the family dog.

Punishment, whether consequential, verbal, or physical, may stop your child from misbehaving at that given moment. However, punishment does very little to prevent temper tantrums or misbehavior, as it does not teach your child skills for safe behavior or self-control.

Mommy Must

Physical punishment takes a toll on your child's emotional development and well-being. Studies show that regularly spanking a child results in their developing a chronic anxiety or fear of being hit. They are also more likely to develop a sense of helplessness and diminished self-esteem.

Chapter 5

If Your Child Puts
on a Show...

WHEN YOUR CHILD ACTS out in public, do you suddenly feel like the victim of every parent's nightmare? It's hard to divert attention away from your screaming, yelling, or thrashing child. It seems like everyone is looking at you, and what you'd like to do is run away and hide, but after all, it's your child and you have to help him calm down. But how? What's the best way to handle this situation and prevent it from happening again? Curbing temper tantrums in public isn't easy, especially since there's extra pressure from an audience you never intended to have. They key is getting down to the right approach for you child, and believe it or not, it can be done!

Why Do Tantrums Happen in Public?

In truth, as a generalization, temper tantrums do not usually happen any more frequently in public than they do at home. Public tantrums may seem to occur more frequently because they are viewed as more memorable. You may not easily recall the fit your child had over his spilled orange juice a few months ago, but the time he threw himself down on the ground screaming at Disneyland is an event no one will forget.

You might be thinking—but my child really does have more tantrums in public! Help! And it's true, some children do tend to have more temper tantrums in public. Even the most serene and even-tempered child may find the stimulation and excitement of some public locales overwhelming. Carnivals, festivals, and even your local supermarket are places with loud noise, bright colors, and plenty of temptations. These factors can lead to a child's feeling stressed or agitated. In addition, other places come with too many adult demands for waiting and being quiet.

Moms Can't Lose Control, Too!

When your child is throwing a tantrum, whether it is at the park, in a restaurant, or in a store, your first

Mindful Mommy
Your adult brain is able to filter out much of the environmental stimuli around you. For example, you can tune out the sound of a barking dog to focus on a television show. But it's not so easy for your young child. Places where she is bombarded with sensory input (loud noises, bright colors, lights, etc.) are more likely to make her feel overwhelmed, agitated, or stressed out.

reaction might be anger. After all, how many times have you tried to talk to your child about why this sort of behavior is inappropriate? You have probably tried to communicate your lack of tolerance for these sort of outbursts, and it might not have been at the best moment—mid-tantrum, for example. Yelling and getting frustrated won't help the situation, either. The angrier you get, the more upset your child will get. How, then, should you go about keeping your temper in check without giving in to your child?

It is normal to be concerned about how onlookers are viewing you. Do you worry that:

- your parenting skills are being judged?
- if you ignore your child, will they think you are being neglectful?
- if you reprimand your child, will they think you are too harsh?
- if you give in, will they think you are spoiling your child?

It may be helpful to realize that at least some of the witnesses have gone through the same thing! These onlookers may empathize with you. In fact, most witnesses are more likely to feel sympathy for you rather than scorn. So don't let yourself get caught up in these worries, and you have a screaming child to worry about anyways!

Although it may be easier said than done, try not worry about what other people think. Just take a deep breath, stay calm, and focus on responding to your child. Pretend that you and your child are alone. Sometimes an onlooker may intervene, either by saying something or by trying to help. Whether they are supportive or critical, it is best to briefly smile at them and then return your focus to your child.

Consistency Is Key!

Recognize that your child can learn to have more temper tantrums in public if you respond to a public temper tantrum differently than you do to one at home. If, to avoid embarrassment or conflict in public, you give in to your child's demands, she will quickly learn that her tantrums are more effective and worthwhile in public. It may be tempting to give in to your child's demands, to avoid the temper tantrum that is bound to follow. Stand your ground and make it clear that her tantrum is not going to get her what she wants.

Consistency is key. So the rule to remember is: Respond to the temper tantrum in public in the same way that you would at home. If you ignore her at home, do the same at the store, even if this means pretending to read a cereal box. You may need to

Mommy Knows Best

Studies show that, regardless of how a parent may respond to a temper tantrum at home, he or she often responds to public temper tantrums in one of two ways. Anger and embarrassment tend to cause parents to either harshly discipline their child or to give in to the child's demands.

move your child to a quiet place, but in the long run, your child will learn there are set expectations for her behavior no matter where she is.

Stopping a Tantrum Before it Starts

Prevention is your first line of defense. You can prevent many problems simply by preparing in advance. Before you step out the door with your child, consider these ways to prevent many temper tantrums before they occur:

Be sure your child is well rested. A tired child is more likely to become cranky. Most young children seem to fare better in the morning because they are more alert and not missing a needed naptime.

Never go hungry. A hungry child is more likely to lose emotional calm and balance, especially in stressful or tiring situations.

Dress your child appropriately. Comfortable clothes and shoes are important. Prepare for those hot stores by dressing your child in easy-to-remove layers. If your child is physically uncomfortable, it is likely that she will be cranky and more prone to having a tantrum.

Make a list. When you have a child who is easily tempted and insists on having everything in the store he sees, try making a shopping list before the trip. Obtain a store flyer and encourage your child to choose one or two items in advance to be added to the list. Be sure to stick to this list in the store!

Review rules in advance. Take time to review with the child what will be happening and how you will expect her to behave.

Choose child-friendly stores. Some stores have removed "high temptation" items like candy and toys from the checkout area, or they have a candy-free checkout aisle.

Other stores have child-sized shopping carts, which help your child feel that she is participating and being a "big" helper, which ultimately prevents her from growing bored, tired, or cranky.

Strategies for Success

As you surely know, not all outings are a walk in the park or a day at the beach. Take heart, there are spe-

Mommy Knows Best

Plan to take your child on errands during off-peak times whenever possible. Grocery stores are often the most chaotic in the early evening and on weekends. Tuesday mornings are ideal. On the other hand, doctor offices seem to be the quietest early in the morning and on Friday afternoons.

cific steps you can take to reduce and manage public meltdowns. The most important thing to remember, as mentioned above, is to stay calm. If you begin to raise your voice or become emotional, chances are your child's behavior will only escalate.

Tips to Prevent a Public Temper Tantrum

Engage your child. Even when the errand is not of interest to him, you can interact with him and keep his interest. Simply ask questions such as, "Who do you think could wear such teeny shoes?" or "How many people can you count in our line?"

Involve him. A child who is involved with the activity is less likely to become bored, restless, or frustrated. You might let him hold the coupon book or sort the items by color. Older children can help bag groceries and may even be able to contribute ideas for the day's agenda.

Have an emergency kit. Bring a little backpack or tote with age-appropriate items for times when your child has to wait or may be restless or cranky. Depending on your child's interests, it may include sticker books, picture books, handheld games, and more. Keep this in your car so it is readily available. Be sure to rotate items to maintain interest.

When Trouble Is Brewing

Respond promptly. It may be easy to react with "just wait until we get home," but this does very little to help a child regain calm and composure. In addition, by the time you get home and address the issue, it is unlikely the child will be able to associate the original behavior with the delayed consequences.

Be flexible. Be in tune with your child's moods and adjust your plans as needed. If you notice your child becoming fidgety in the shoe store, take a brief walk around the mall or stop for a pretzel before venturing on to the next store. Other early signs of trouble include increased crankiness and whining.

Offer a snack. Even a small snack boosts blood sugar levels, energy, and mood. Keep a hidden stash of breadsticks or granola bars in your purse or glove compartment for a quick snack anytime.

Make concessions. Not everything has to be an all-or-nothing battle. Sometimes offering a limited

Mindful Mommy

Many malls and larger stores now have supervised play or activity areas set up. Such a place may be very welcome for your bored or restless child and a needed break for you.

choice breaks the cycle of power struggles. For example, "Although I can't let you have every toy you see, you may choose one doll if you walk through the rest of the store nicely with me."

Avoid leaving. Use the above strategies to help your child regain control. Do not simply give up on the errand or leave the location unless necessary. If you leave a location as soon as your child has a tantrum, she will quickly learn to manipulate you to avoid going to unpleasant places such as the doctor's office.

Find a refuge. When your child is having a full-fledged temper tantrum, take her to a quiet area away from the center of activity and traffic until you can help her calm down and regain control.

Avoid Touchy Situations

Beyond the general guidelines, there are specific ways you can cope with your child's temper tantrums in a variety of settings. Each location or situation comes with its own set of potential challenges or problems that you may need to respond to.

Think ... Takeout

Restaurants are a common setting for temper tantrums. You are probably asking your child to meet higher behavioral expectations than you would in the more informal home setting. Home may have a different set of rules. For example:

- At home, you may allow her to leave the table when finished, or to get up and serve herself.

BUT

- In a restaurant, you ask your child to sit still, wait quietly, and exhibit his best manners, all while being hungry.

In order to keep your little one entertained, there are some very simple things that you can do. You can cut down on the waiting time for your hungry child. Ask your waitress to bring rolls or an appetizer once you are seated. Buffets are ideal, and they have the added benefit of giving your child the chance to walk around a bit (with your supervision) and reduce her fidgetiness. When your child does have a temper tantrum, you will probably need to leave the table. Retreat to the restroom or lobby with your child. Keep in mind the others in the restaurant—don't ruin their meal too!

If your child always seems hungry and impatient when you are waiting at a restaurant, pack a little snack that your child can munch on while she waits.

Just Sit and Wait

Doctor's offices and waiting rooms can be difficult places for a young child to remain calm and in control. Here again, you are asking your child to sit still and be quiet. Waiting rooms are notoriously uncomfortable places to be—the chairs are hard, the lights are harsh, and other people waiting may be uncomfortable or distraught. Unless you are in a pediatrician's office, it is unlikely there will be any toys, books, or pleasant distractions for your child. To make matters worse, your child may be ill or feeling anxious about the impending appointment. If your child has a meltdown, you may want to approach the receptionist. She may be able to delay your appointment until your child is calm. Conversely, if your child's temper tantrum is because of impatience, she may be able to arrange for you to be waited on sooner. It does not hurt to ask. Be sure to let her know if you are going to remove the child. Sometimes a trip to the water fountain or a brief stroll around the building will provide the distraction your child needs.

To Market, to Market

A trip to the store can be challenging for a child. Shopping is simply not a fun activity for a young child. For what is usually an extended period, you are asking your child to either walk nicely by your side

Mommy Knows Best

Look for restaurants that are child friendly. Many restaurants now do several things to accommodate families with young children. Some restaurants provide puzzle place mats, tablecloths that can be colored, or even tabletop toys.

or to remain in a cart. They may see many attractive items that they find tempting but are not allowed to touch or have them. Remember that stores are often hot, crowded, and noisy, adding to a child's irritability and yours as well.

One mother shares:

My daughter was a reasonably calm and well-behaved child. This all changed when I would take her shopping for school clothes. I knew I could expect that, sometime during the day, she would become agitated and whiny and eventually have a full screaming tantrum in the middle of the dressing room. I was perplexed that she had no problems at grocery or hardware stores. Finally, it occurred to me to ask her if she knew why the department store made her feel so out of control. It turns out that she was getting static shocks from the clothing racks as she brushed by them, and then she was stepping on pins left on the dressing room floor! We started to shop at another store and she was fine.

When Fun Places Are Not Fun

If your child has a temper tantrum at a fair, amusement park, or carnival, one of your first concerns needs to be safety. When your young child has a meltdown in one of these places, there is a risk that your child will run from you and be lost in the crowd or injured. If your child is losing control, your first step is to contain her. Get her to sit down on a bench or lead her over to a pavilion. If you determine that overexcitement and over-stimulation are playing a part, find a place or activity for calming down. Many amusement parks offer more sedate activities that can be restful for both of you. Take a break from the wild rides and loud music and explore the surrounding gardens or the paddleboats on the lake. It is helpful to note, when your child has a temper tantrum in a "fun" place, leaving will not reinforce her tantrum and it may be an effective way to prevent further problems.

Visiting Friends and Family

Before visiting other people's homes, be sure to define the rules clearly to your child. Inform him of any special restrictions in advance. Can he pet the dog? Are there off-limits items in the host's house? If your child has a temper tantrum, calmly excuse yourself and your child to the bathroom or porch and help your child regain control. If your child is unable to calm down, you may need to end the visit.

Mommy Must

When in public, find a refuge—a quiet area away from the center of activity and traffic. If you determine your child is having an attention-seeking tantrum, calmly tell him you will wait for him to stop before returning to the activity. If your child is having a tantrum for a developmental reason (frustration, poor verbal skills), patiently comfort him and address the issue at hand.

Enjoying the Fine Arts

If your child has a tantrum in a movie theater, everyone around you will know. More than likely, your child's tantrum will be a disruption to the other theatergoers. Recognize that your child may be more likely to act up if the movie content is scary or too mature for her. Immediately take your child to a quiet space such as the bathroom or the lobby to regain control. Allow your child time to settle down completely. Be sure she is ready to go back into the theater. If you suspect that the problem will continue, it may be best to leave. Young children often enjoy live theater more than movies. Many cities have a children's theater program geared toward young children. These productions are usually lively and interactive, which helps engage children and make them less likely to become upset.

Going for a Ride

Maybe the worst place for a temper tantrum is on mass transit. You and your child are taking an eight-hour bus ride or flight to visit Grandma. Your child's toy rolls under the seat and it is not retrievable. Predictably, your child goes into hysterics. There are very few places to take your child aside. Whether you are taking the crosstown bus or a transatlantic flight, be sure to bring some activities or books. It may help if you can get a seat by the window. If your child has a tantrum, you may need to find refuge in the bathroom or in the back row of seats. If you are truly stuck, you can try holding him or rubbing his back.

One mother faced with this situation came up with a creative idea. She draped a travel blanket over them both. This gave them some privacy. It also helped her out-of-control toddler to focus on her efforts to calm him down.

Public tantrums can, indeed, be particularly troublesome. However, as with tantrums at home, your calm and consistent response will result in diminishing displays of public temper tantrums.

Chapter 6

Other Caregivers and Your Child— A Recipe for Disaster?

DOES THIS SOUND FAMILIAR? You have devoted a lot of effort to curbing your child's temper tantrums at home. You feel that you have made great strides in helping your child develop self-control and manage strong emotions such as anger and frustration. *But* the calm that you established exists only when your child is with you. When your child is with Grandma or at child care, she is still having many temper tantrums. How can you work with other caregivers and help them cope with your child's temper tantrums when you are not present?

How Your Child Behaves With Others

Your child may actually have more temper tantrums when he is with you than when he is with others. This is actually quite common and you should not take it personally. First, remember that you have probably directly taught your child to behave a certain way with other adults. Their behavior around other caregivers may be controlled and constricted. When your child is with you, he is comfortable and free to fully be himself. Your child trusts you and knows it is safe to "let it all hang out." He can feel secure in knowing that you will accept him, love him, and keep him safe, even if he loses control.

A good example of this can be seen with three-year-old Katie. It was clear to Katie's preschool teacher that Katie was unhappy being away from Mom and that she was reluctant to participate in preschool activities. However, Katie did not cry or whine for her mother. Rather, she was sullen, quiet, and somewhat withdrawn. When Katie's mother came to pick her up, Katie fell to pieces. She was crying so hard that her mother mistakenly thought that Katie was not glad to see her. To the contrary, now Katie felt safe to let go of the strong emotions that she was holding in all day.

Your child is bound to behave differently for other people. This is human nature. You act differently

Mindful Mommy

You will probably not be able to predict how your child will behave when you leave her in the care of another adult. Even if your child appears to listen and respect that person in your presence, your child's behavior may be very different once you have gone.

depending on where you are or whom you are interacting with, don't you? Of course! You behave very differently when you are at work, interacting with a client, than you do when you are at home alone with your spouse. The same will be true for your child. In fact, you probably encourage it. It is likely that you have encouraged your child, from a very early age, to behave differently in public than he does at home. You may urge your child to use "their special manners" when Aunt Carol comes for a visit.

Behave Yourself

Generally, most parents take active steps to help their child learn to interact with others appropriately. Oftentimes, these standards of behavior are more stringent than they are for behavior at home. You may teach your child very specific manners or codes of conduct. For example, "Address other adults by their last name" or "When we visit Grammy, we have to remember to sit only on the plastic-covered couch."

Tantrums with Others

Your child may be more likely to exhibit misbehavior or have temper tantrums while in the care of another adult. This may be true for all other adults or just a select few. Surely, the unique and personal interaction that these adults and your child share will affect your child's behavior. However, these are a few general reasons why your child my have more temper tantrums while she is in the care of another adult. Let's take a look:

Stress

Stress may be a strong reason for your child's temper tantrums. This may be particularly true if your child does not know the caregiver well. The child may also feel additional stress if the caregiving is to happen in an unfamiliar place. You may be able to avoid some problems by simply requesting that the adult care for your child in your home rather than in their home.

Separation and Favoritism

Whether your child knows the caregiver well or not, do not discount the possibility of separation anxiety. Some children may even have difficulty being left alone with a close family member.

Testing Limits

While you have been raising and disciplining your child, you have been setting down clear expectations and parameters for their behavior. Children need the sense of security of knowing that some-

Mommy Knows Best

You can minimize the potential for your child to have temper tantrums with other caregivers by limiting the number of people who care for your child. The more stability there is for your child, the less stress and uncertainty he faces. Children will have more emotional maturity and control when they can form close attachments with a select few consistent caregivers.

one will limit their behavior and keep them safe. Children also need to learn by direct experience what those limits are and what the consequences are for exceeding those limits. You may or may not have gone through a stage with your child where she is actively testing the limits. Regardless, your child may be compelled to reenter the process with every new caregiver. She may be thinking things like, "Okay, I know that I must pick up my toys at home, but what about at day care?" "Daddy won't let me watch cartoons, but maybe the babysitter will." "Mom ignores me when I scream for a cookie, but I wonder if Grandma will give in."

There will be unavoidable times when you will need to have someone care for your child. Whether this is a onetime event of a few hours or a full-time arrangement, your child may have increased difficulty maintaining emotional control, and therefore, she will be more prone to temper tantrums. Whenever possible, prepare your child in advance. Let her know what will be happening and what she can expect. Be very clear and specific about how you expect her to behave in these situations. Avoid vague directives like "be nice at child care" or "don't misbehave for Aunt Nancy." Tell your child in a positive way exactly what you expect her to do: "When you are at child care, I want you to use your words if you are angry with other children." "Follow your aunt Nancy's rules and pet her dog gently."

It's All Relative

It is likely that there will be a time when a family member will care for your child. This may occur on an as-needed basis or perhaps he or she will be caring for your child every day. There are both pros and cons to having a relative provide child care for your child.

You do need to consider if this person is the best person to care for your child. Here are some questions to ask:

- Is this person patient with children?
- Is she physically able to chase or carry a young child, if needed?
- Will she supervise your young child at all times?
- Does she have experience with or knowledge of child development and guidance?
- Can she keep your child safe and healthy? (CPR and first-aid training are desirable.)

Do You Enlist Relative Help on a Regular Basis?

There are many reasons why relative child care may be the best option for your family. Relative care

Mommy Knows Best

Relative child care is still very popular. At one time or another, upward of 45 percent of all parents will call on a family member to care for their child. In rural areas where child care programs are scarce, as many as 75 percent of parents will choose a relative for child care.

may be the most convenient and accessible option, especially if the caregiver will be someone who lives in the child's home or nearby. Relative child care may be the option that you feel the most comfortable with. Perhaps the only person you will trust with the care of your child is your own mother. You can be assured that your child will receive more individualized attention than he would at a child care center. Finally, you may have more flexibility with both cost and scheduling when making child care arrangements with a family member.

Specific Issues to Keep in Mind

When a relative is caring for your child, there may be specific issues that arise that can lead to your child's having a temper tantrum. Most problems will occur because there is a lack of consistency between your child-rearing philosophy and approach and that of the relative caregiver. Almost any difference between the way you and the relative interact with your child can open the door for her to test limits. An older child in particular will look for exceptions and caveats to the rules that she may have at home. By establishing consistent discipline policies that match what you do at home, you can avoid the famous whine, "But Grandma lets me . . . "

A relative caregiver may wish to ensure that the child has fun and enjoys his company. Therefore, he may feel guilty or reluctant to enforce the rules and limits that you have set. Reassure him that there are ways that he can "spoil" or "treat" your child without allowing the child to break or bend the guidelines you have set for appropriate behavior.

Consistency Among Caregivers

There is one best way to prevent and manage your child's temper tantrums when they're with another caregiver: consistency. Your child needs to know that your expectations for her behavior do not change. Temper tantrums will be responded to in the same fashion, all of the time. For example, you decided that you will ignore your child when she has a temper tantrum because she wants a cookie before dinner. This means that you will ignore her if this happens at the store and that you will ignore her if this happens at the neighbor's annual barbecue picnic. This also means that your neighbors will ignore the tantrum and so will Grandpa and Uncle Bobby. Once there is a broken link in the chain, there will be a problem. If Uncle Bobby gives in to your child's tantrum just once, you can surely expect that your child's temper tantrum behavior will increase when she visits Uncle Bobby.

Mommy Knows Best

In spite of your best efforts, you may find that the grandparents are overly judgmental or critical about the way that you are managing your child's behavior. If it is clear that you cannot establish a consistent approach for your child or you doubt that they will honor your wishes, then you should consider finding a new caregiver for your child.

Before a relative cares for your child, even if only for a few hours, it is wise to communicate clearly to her how you manage and guide your child's behavior and temper tantrums.

Challenges with Grandparents

The most common and popular relative child care arrangement is with your child's grandparents. Along with the special joy that may come with intergenerational care, there are unique challenges regarding establishing discipline policies for your own child.

Most grandparents will have an opinion on how you should raise your children and manage their behavior. They will usually feel like they have some competence and expertise on the matter; after all, look how good you turned out! Remember, grandparents' concerns and opinions are usually a sign that they feel love and commitment to you and your child.

It is normal that you may feel uncomfortable sharing parenting strategies with in-laws or your own parents. If you are using a different approach than they did, you may worry that you are offending or hurting them. It is possible that you will feel judged or scrutinized for your own parenting abilities as well. It may be helpful to remind yourself that, in this situation, you are both an adult and the parent.

Tips to Reach Agreement

There are specific ways that you can communicate with grandparents as you establish a consistent approach to your child's behavior. Use humor when you can. Find common ground by asking Grandma to share some stories of your worst temper tantrums.

Nowadays, when parents look for child-rearing advice, they turn to doctors, books, or the Internet. Do not forget that grandparents have a wealth of experience and will want to feel valued. When possible, involve them in decision making. Do not be afraid to ask them for advice, but remember that you are not obligated to take it.

Set up a specific plan for managing your child's behavior in advance. Be sure to review strategies that you use at home for preventing temper tantrums, such as avoiding fatigue, hunger, and over-stimulating places.

Here is just a partial list of possible situations you may wish to plan for. Decide together how grandparents should respond to the child when:

- She cries when you leave
- He grabs a toy from another child
- She has a meltdown because a toy is too difficult for her
- He gets angry and bites his cousin

Mindful Mommy

Although you ideally want consistency between you and the caregiver, when managing your child's behavior, not everything has to be the same. Grandparents do not have to follow every rule you have to a T. It is okay if they allow your child some special privileges or choose to impose their own house rules as well.

- She has a tantrum when it is time for a nap
- He screams and kicks when Grandpa will not buy him a toy at the store
- She gets frustrated when trying to put on her shoes

Describe in detail how you want the grandparents to respond to your child's temper tantrums. Be specific and try to cover all of the possible scenarios. At home, you may respond very differently to a temper tantrum that is caused by fear than a temper tantrum that is staged to get your attention.

Daycare Dilemmas

Anyone who cares for your child for any length of time will have an impact on his development and behavior. Therefore, you will want to use great care in selecting a child care provider. Ideally, you want to find someone who will work together with you to guide and teach your child.

There are many child care options to consider. Each one has its drawbacks and its benefits. Only you can

Mommy Must

You want to make sure that the program you choose is licensed or registered. This tells you that the program meets minimum standards of health and safety. Programs that received accreditation have met even higher standards of quality.

choose what is the best option for both you and your child. Here are the most popular child care options.

Nannies

A nanny may live in or out of your home. With a nanny, you will have the most influence and control over your child's care. You will be able to dictate all policies and rules as you choose. A nanny will be exclusively devoted to the care of only your child. Keep in mind that a nanny may not have the same level of education and training as family or center care providers, and nannies are usually the most expensive child care option.

Family Day Care Providers

A family day care provider takes children into her home, usually while she is caring for her own children. She may be either registered or licensed by the state. The group size will be smaller than a center program but will often be a mixed age group. Infants through school age will be all together. Consequently, your toddler could be with a group of four- and five-year-olds, or your school-ager may be spending his day with infants and toddlers. A family day care provider may be flexible regarding your requests, but it is wise to be sure that you agree on basic child guidance and discipline approaches before enrolling your child.

Center Programs

If you want your child to have experience interacting and playing with children her own age, then a child care center may be the best bet. Because child care centers are the most regulated, staff and teachers are most likely to have the highest level of training and education in child development and behavior. Child care centers are also the most likely to provide your child with enrichment and school readiness activities. On the other hand, large group size means less individualized attention for your child. Recognize that you will have considerably less influence over the program's policies, so it will be up to you to find a program that suits you and your child.

Before Starting Child Care

Before enrolling your child with a child care provider or hiring a nanny, sit down and discuss your values and beliefs about child rearing and guidance with them. Also, take the time to listen to his or her approach to managing children's behavior. You will find as many different approaches as there are providers. You want someone who basically agrees with your approach and, more importantly, is willing to work with you as a partner to provide consistent care for your child.

Get to Know the Provider

Ask the provider how she manages children's behavior, how she uses discipline, and how she responds to temper tantrums. Because they are usually caring for groups of children rather than one child, family day care providers and center providers will typically respond to temper tantrums in a slightly different way than you do at home.

Because the child care provider has a background in child development as well as managing groups of children, a majority of her behavioral management techniques will be focused on prevention. Room arrangement, daily scheduling, and seating plans are things that she will consider as she strives to prevent misbehavior and temper tantrums.

She may ignore minor upsets and temper tantrums, often encouraging older children to resolve conflicts with only some minor guidance or intervention. When things get out of hand and children become aggressive, she may use time-out more than you would at home. This may simply be because it is the most effective way for her to keep all of the children safe and in control.

Share about Your Child

In order to make sure that you and the child care provider agree on how to manage your child's temper tantrums, take the time to share your views and information about your child. It will be beneficial if you share with the provider specific information about your child's temper tantrums. Here are possible things to mention:

- Known triggers
- Problematic times of the day
- Your child's verbal skills

- The impact of hunger or fatigue on your child's behavior
- How your child manages strong emotions such as anger and frustration
- What calms your child
- How you respond to temper tantrums at home

New Triggers and Challenges for Your Child

Once your child is in a child care setting, you may witness temper tantrums as a result of new issues or triggers that are associated with the child care experience. Remember, you are asking your child to adapt to a new environment, new people, and a new schedule all at once. If your child is slow to adapt, you are bound to witness your child having difficulty early on.

Also remember, your child will be facing a new set of expectations, limits, and guidelines. It may be difficult for your child to learn the following: in child care, I am allowed to ____, but at home, I cannot ____. Your child may also feel some stress as she

Mindful Mommy

Child care turnover affects young children. Young children will become attached to their caregivers in much the same way that they do with their parents. The departure of a caregiver can be very upsetting and stressful. Studies show that when infants and toddlers go through many providers, they tend to perform less well in preschool.

tries to get used to a more structured daily schedule. Additionally, a brightly colored, ornately decorated, busy, and noisy classroom may be over-stimulating for your child.

One of the biggest benefits to enrolling your child in a child care center is that she will have opportunities to interact with other children her own age. This will help promote her language skills as well as important social skills, including cooperation, negotiation, conflict resolution, and sharing. If your child is prone to temper tantrums because she is egocentric or she has difficulty sharing, interacting with other children in a group setting may be particularly helpful in eventually helping your child build skills to overcome those problems. This will not happen overnight, though. Be aware that if your child has not had much exposure to other children her own age, you may initially see an increase in her temper tantrums as she begins to learn to adapt her behavior to meet the expectations for group interactions and dynamics.

Don't Leave Me! Separation Anxiety

Possibly the most common cause of temper tantrums with a child care provider will be separation anxiety. Separation anxiety and tantrums will be most prevalent for children ages ten months to three years of age, children who have never been away from you, and children who are not securely attached to you.

You can read more about the causes for separation anxiety in chapter 8.

Make a Plan

Work together with your child care provider. She deals with this issue on almost a daily basis, and together you should be able to devise a strategy that will make good-byes an easier time for all of you. Do not wait for the first separation temper tantrum. There are things you can do to prevent problems. Prepare your child in advance; tell him what will be happening and what he can expect. Make the transition gradual. Arrange to visit the program with your child at least once; let him tour the room and meet the teacher. Whenever possible, spend a little time in the program with your child for the first few days. Avoid just rushing out the door.

Time to Say Good-bye

You may find it helpful if you establish a good-bye routine and then stick with it. Perhaps you will always help her hang up her jacket, give her a hug, and once inside the classroom, wave at her through the door. Avoid lingering or going back for "just one

Mommy Knows Best

There are some wonderful children's books that you can choose to read to your child to help prepare her. Here are some good ones to start with: *Adam's Daycare* by Julie Ovenell-Carter, *Carl Goes to Daycare* by Alexandra Day, and *Going to Daycare* by Fred Rogers.

more hug." In the long run, this makes good-byes even more difficult.

Although this separation may be difficult for you as well, stay positive. Avoid dramatizing the event with statements like, "Oh, sweetie, I am so, so sorry I have to leave you here!" Instead, paint the picture in a positive way by saying something like, "While I am at work today, you will be able to stay in the fun school and play with other children." Do not forget to reassure your child that he can always count on the fact that you will be returning for him. It may be helpful if you can give him a concrete idea of when to expect you: "I will pick you up right after snacktime."

Chapter 7

Top Tantrum
Prevention Techniques

THE TRUTH IS THAT temper tantrums are a normal part of your young child's behavior, unfortunately. You will most likely encounter several tantrums during the early years and it is unrealistic to expect that you will be able to prevent them all! You can, however, recognize some of the common triggers and causes of many of your child's temper tantrums. Once you can identify potential causes, you can prevent many tantrums before they happen.

Limits and Rules Lead
to Less Tantrums

The more self-control your child has, the less likely she will be to have temper tantrums. Self-control allows your child to regulate and control her emotions. Learning self-control is an ongoing process that occurs with your support and discipline. Your child needs limits and external boundaries in order for her to internalize rules and standards of behavior that will allow her to develop self-control.

Children Need Limits, Believe It or Not!

Your child has a deep-rooted need for limits on his behavior. The limits and boundaries that you set for your child's behavior will make him feel secure. Some children will directly ask for guidance or limits if they feel they need them. This is particularly true when a child is in a new situation where there may be less structure and fewer rules. A child who is raised with a lot of structure and rules may enter a more lax environment and start to ask, "Is it okay if I . . . ?" "Are we allowed to . . . ?" You may even witness your child putting himself in time-out when he gets upset. He may ask you what is allowed or acceptable in a given situation. He needs to know that an adult is there to guide him and keep him safe and in control. When he is feeling confused, scared, frustrated, angry, or overwhelmed, he will count on you to guide him with authority and control.

Mommy Must

Setting limits and boundaries on your child's behavior does not mean taking away her freedom or autonomy. You can still allow your child to have many choices within the parameters that you set. For example, "Playing ball in the street is not safe. You can play ball or another game that you choose, but you must stay in the yard."

No Rules?

If you choose to set very few or no limitations on your child's behavior, she will have a difficult time learning safe, appropriate behavior and self-control. You are handing over to your child the control to regulate her own behavior. This parenting style or approach is known as permissive parenting. Permissive parents will usually establish very few rules and often do not consistently enforce the rules that they have set. Due to a lack of your child's experience, and her cognitive and emotional immaturity, this approach is rarely effective and is bound to be a disaster. Can you imagine what would happen if you said to your toddler, "I have laid out your pajamas for you. I trust you to know when you are tired. You can decide when you are ready to go to bed." Or, "I see that your teeth are bothering you. Let me know if you wish to go to the dentist."

When your child fails at regulating her own behavior, she will be more likely to have outbursts and temper tantrums and to lose her self-control. She will not be making independent decisions. Eventually, she will rely on others to control her decisions and actions. If you do not set and enforce limits for her, school or law authorities may need to do so later on in her life.

High Expectations, Too High?

By establishing rules, you are setting limits and parameters for your child's safe and acceptable behavior. These rules should become guidelines that clearly communicate your expectations. When you establish rules for your child, there are many things to consider.

Who Writes the Rules?

Obviously, when your child is very young, you will take sole responsibility for establishing all rules and codes of conduct. Once your child is past three years old, you should consider involving her when you are generating the rules. There are many benefits to involving your child. If she is involved in a discussion about potential rules, she will be more likely to understand their importance. She will be more likely to comply with rules she thought of and agreed with. Additionally, she will be less likely to view rules as arbitrary or unfair.

If contributing to the household rules is a difficult task for your young child, try to make it more concrete and realistic. Take a piece of poster board and draw a line down the middle. Label one column "DO" and the other column "DON'T." Ask your child what he can do to be safe, for items to put in the "DO" column, and what is not safe or nice behavior, for the "DON'T" column. Try to draft your list of rules mainly from the "DO" list and state the rules in a positive way.

There are three difficulties that may arise when you try to involve your older child in generating a rule list:

- She may not wish to participate. If this is the case, just go ahead and create the list without her.
- She creates too many detailed rules. For example, "No bouncing tennis balls in the house. No kicking soccer balls in the house. No rolling balls down the steps." If this happens, help her create a more general rule: "All ball playing stays outside."
- She creates rules that are unreasonable or impossible for everyone to adhere to. For example, "Everyone can have only four ounces of water to drink before bedtime. Only children older than five can watch TV. You must brush your teeth each and every time you eat chocolate or anything brown." If this occurs, ask your child to consider the fairness of the rule and if she will truly be able and willing to follow it herself.

Clarity Is Key!

The rules should be a clear statement of your expectations for your child's behavior. Rules should be brief and to the point. Avoid rules that include exceptions and variable factors. Here is an example of such a rule: "Don't stay out past 8 p.m. on school nights unless you already have permission or you call before 7 p.m. to ask for this time to be extended. Both parents must agree that you may stay out later than

8 p.m., unless one parent cannot be reached before 7:30 p.m. If only one parent is contacted, you must return home by 8:30 p.m. to secure further permission." Not only is this rule confusing, but it leaves a lot of room for your child to attempt to negotiate for leniency.

Sweet and Specific Expectations

Do not expect your child to be a mind reader. State your expectations very specifically. Parents often just tell children directives such as "be nice," "be good for Grandma," and "don't act up!" Remember that your standards or ideals of what is "well behaved" will probably be vastly different from what your child considers "well behaved." When you tell your ten-year-old that you want his room to be clean, you are envisioning a room where all of the books are lined up in alphabetical order, the bed is made with fresh sheets, and his floor is mopped and waxed. Conversely, your ten-year-old believes a clean room to be a room where all of the dirty laundry is hidden under the bed. Other examples of vague rule statements include "calm down" and "help out."

State Rules Positively

Rules should state what behavior you expect. Tell your child what to do. Avoid negatively phrased rules. Younger children, in particular, will focus on the action and disregard the negation. For example, when you tell your preschooler, "Do not go near the swimming pool without an adult," he focuses on the phrase "go near the swimming pool." "Stop pulling the cat's tail" becomes "pull the cat's tail." You can change a rule from negative to positive just by changing a few words. Like this:

Negative Rules	Become Positive Rules
No running in the house.	Walk while you are in the house.
You may not eat in the living room.	Food stays in the kitchen.
Candy before dinner is not allowed.	Candy is allowed only after dinner.
No watching TV before your homework is done.	Do your homework before you watch TV.

If you look at the negative rules above, you can see how ambiguous they can be, especially to a child who is testing limits. When you say, "No running in the house," your child may ask, "What about galloping, sprinting, or spinning?" When you say, "You may not eat in the living room," they may ask, "What about my bedroom?" Notice how the positive rules are clear and defined, leaving less room for questioning.

Mindful Mommy

Toddlers can be very literal and rigid when they hear and interpret rules. When you say, "Food stays in the kitchen," your toddler may insist that Spike's food bowls be brought up from the garage.

Choosing Rules

Although you want your expectations to be clear, it is neither wise nor practical to list a rule for every possible infraction. First, you will never be able to anticipate all of your child's future misbehaviors. Second, you will end up with a list of rules more lengthy and complex than the federal tax code. Consider your priorities. Pick just a few clear and easy-to-remember rules that you feel will serve as guidelines in helping your child learn safe behavior and self-control. Consider your child's developmental abilities. Make sure the rules reflect reasonable expectations for her age and maturity.

For example, requiring your three-year-old to make her bed independently each and every morning is a rule that will be difficult for her to comply with. If you want your child to remember and internalize your rules, try to keep the list short. For children under school age, three to five rules are optimal. Even for older children, it is best to keep the lists short.

Follow These Three Basic Rules

To keep expectations simple, you can set a few broad rules that can encompass your expectations of your child's behavior. Here are three suggested rules. You will find they are clear, easy to remember, and will cover just about any misbehavior you would want to respond to.

Be Safe to Others

"Others" can include friends, family member, pets, and so forth. Unsafe behaviors include hitting, biting, grabbing, and teasing or name-calling (which "hurts" feelings). You may wish to explain to your child that you will not allow anyone to hurt him and you will not allow him to hurt others. You will also refer to the rule if he is hurting you.

Be Safe to Yourself

You can remind your child that it is important to you that he stay safe and healthy. This rule includes all behaviors that are unsafe to the child (running with scissors, playing in the busy street) and can also include behaviors that protect his health (hand washing, eating nutritious foods).

Be Safe to Things

You are asking your child to respect all toys, materials, and property. Behaviors that fall under this rule include breaking toys and coloring on walls. You can refer to this rule the next time your toddler dumps all of your papers out of your briefcase!

You, an Enforcer

How you respond to misbehavior and how you enforce limits will send strong messages to your child. You are showing her what behavior you expect and value. You are showing her that she can depend on you to help her regain and maintain control when she is acting out or having a temper tantrum.

Make a Priority List

Focus your enforcement on the rules that are most important in helping your child learn safe behavior and self-control. It is okay to allow some minor infractions. For the sake of your own sanity, pick your battles and do not sweat the small stuff. Perhaps, you want your child to eat nutritious food at every meal. Dinnertime rolls around and you become locked in a battle with your child. You are planning to serve peas but she wants asparagus instead. In the grand scheme of things, will it really matter if she has asparagus instead of peas? In fact, if your ultimate motivation is her health, a few meals without a vegetable serving at all will do no harm. Do not let the original rules or intent get lost in a battle of wills.

Reasonable Rule?

Always try to state the reason for a rule as you enforce it. Your explanation does not need to be a lengthy lecture; a brief statement will do. For example, "Put your feet on the floor. It is not safe for you

Mommy Knows Best

Almost any misbehavior you will encounter will fall under the three basic rules. Behaviors that do no harm, directly or indirectly, are often best ignored. These behaviors include tattling, whining, pouting, and bathroom or silly talk. In fact, responding to these types of behaviors will usually increase their frequency.

to climb on the railing. You could fall." "Return the scissors to their case so no one gets stabbed by them." When you state the reason for a rule, your child will be less likely to see the rule as arbitrary or as just your way of exerting power. Explanation statements such as "Because I am the dad" or "Because I said so" are statements that will surely be met with resistance by your child and do not teach anything.

Most importantly, when you repeatedly state the reason for a rule, you are helping your child learn the consequences of his actions, and you are promoting the development of his inner voice or conscience. Let's take a look at a real life example:

Your five-year-old keeps jumping on your bed. Each time you catch her, you tell her, "Stop jumping on my bed." When she whines, "But why?" you snap, "Because I say stop. Now go outside to play and do not let me catch you jumping on the bed again." She obediently leaves, but only until she sees that you are in the laundry room and she does not think you will catch her. She continues to sneak into your room and jump on your bed. Then you read this book. The next time you see her jumping on the bed, you say, "I want you to stop jumping on my bed. It is not safe. You could bounce off and hit your head. If you want to jump safely, go outside." The next time she approaches your bed, there is a good chance she will stop and think, "Even if I will not be caught, it is a bad idea for me to jump on the bed. I do not want to hit my head." She has now begun to internalize the rule and develop self-control. Finally, it is important to note that, if you are unable to explain or justify a rule, you should reconsider whether it is a fair or reasonable rule.

Stay Consistent!

You are the enforcer now, and always (until your little one grows up at least)! As your child is learning what it is that you expect from him, he is also learning what to expect from you. Consistently respond and enforce the limits and rules that you have set. Lax enforcement of your rules is no better than not having any rules at all. For example, you have told your child that he may not play in the living room. The last few times you found him playing there, you removed the toys he was playing with and sent him to his room. However, on one occasion, you were in the middle of cooking dinner and it had been a hectic day for you. You decided to let this misbehavior slide, just once, promising yourself that you will be sure to punish him for both offenses the next time you see him. The problem is, your child may interpret this by thinking he can get away with the misbehavior

Mindful Mommy

Tell your child the potential consequences of her actions: "If you throw those blocks one more time, I will put them away." However, it is critical that you follow through. If not, your child will quickly learn to disregard your threats in much the same way the village disregarded the boy who cried wolf.

whenever you are busy or harried. Additionally, with rare exception, a rule should apply no matter where the child is, what time of day it is, or who is enforcing the rule. If not, your child will quickly learn that rules she can bend are the easiest rules to break.

And so, if Dad allows your child to stay up later than you do, there may be conflict. Your child may even learn to play one parent against the other. You will find that the most effective way to change and influence your child's behavior is to have all caregivers respond to and manage your child's behavior in a set and consistent fashion. In chapter 9, you will find tips for working with other relatives and child care providers for this very objective.

Can It Be Stress?

It is easy to view childhood as a carefree time, a time of lots of freedom and few worries or responsibilities. The truth is, you cannot completely shelter your child from the up-and-down stresses of daily life. Even in the most idyllic childhood, there is disappointment and loss. As it is with adults, stress affects a child's demeanor and behavior. A child who is experiencing stress is far more likely to be irritable, oversensitive, and prone to temper tantrums. Although you cannot remove all stress from your child's life, you can buffer him from its effects. You can reduce many temper tantrums simply by recognizing that he is feeling stress, and responding to him with empathy.

Stress Can Come at an Early Age

Many things could be stressful for your child. Realize that each child is different, and some children are more resilient than others. For example, one child may react to the death of a pet goldfish by calmly requesting a trip to the pet store for a replacement. Another grieving child may be inconsolable, vowing to never love another animal for as long as she lives. There is a long list of events or experiences that may prove stressful for your child. A few of these include illness, divorce, moving, death of a family member, new school, a fight with a sibling, losing a favorite toy, or nightmares. In fact, just about any change in your child's life or routine may be stressful.

Signs of Stress

Each child will exhibit stress in a different way. Observe your child carefully. Changes in her habits or routines are often a strong indicator that she is experiencing stress.

Here are some common signs of stress in young children:

Mindful Mommy

Positive occurrences can also be stressful for your child. Many of these events are preceded by a lot of anticipation and excitement, which can be overwhelming for a young child. A few of the events include holiday celebrations, birthdays, vacation travel, and starting school.

Change in sleep habits. Your child starts having difficulty falling asleep at night, or maybe she is beginning to wake up in the middle of the night. She may start grinding her teeth. Nightmares or night terrors may become more frequent.

Change in eating habits. You may notice that your child suddenly becomes finicky at mealtimes. If he is stressed, his appetite could either decrease or increase.

Change in social interactions. Your once popular child is having difficulties interacting with others. Perhaps she has become sullen or defiant. She may become more aggressive or have a hard time sustaining play activities.

Change in mood or personality. Your once cheerful, independent child has become overly sensitive, demanding, or clingy.

Change in other habits. Your child may exhibit other signs of stress, including stuttering, nail biting, hair twirling, regression, or self-stimulation.

One mother shares how she finally recognized that her three-year-old son was experiencing stress:

I thought I had it all under control. When I was preparing to have my second child, I spent a lot of time preparing Trevor for the arrival of the baby.

I read books to him and involved him in picking out the baby furniture, the whole nine yards. He seemed as excited as everyone else waiting for the baby to be born. He seemed thrilled when I finally brought his little sister home from the hospital. He never said anything negative and he still maintained a cheery attitude like normal. Nevertheless, I did start to notice something odd. He was starting to act more and more like a baby himself. He started to insist that he also drink out of a bottle. Then, what really made me realize he was not as happy as he seemed, was when, after seven months without a problem, he started to pee his bed again!

Responding to a Stressed Child

The way you respond to your child gives you the ability to alleviate much of your child's stress. First, if you are able, eliminate or reduce the source of your child's stress. Be sure to respond to your child with compassion and empathy. Listen carefully to her concerns. Acknowledge her feelings with statements like, "I can see that you are upset because your friend is moving" or "I understand how much the upcoming math test is worrying you."

Know what is calming for your child. If touch is calming for him, try hugs, massages, or even a warm bath. If activity is calming for him, try some silly dancing or go for a long walk together. Recognize that what may be soothing for one child may be agitating for another. Rollicking rock music may help one child calm down and yet be too stimulating for another.

Prepare for Stress

Since change is a common stress for young children, whenever possible, prepare your child in advance. Imagine the shock you would feel if you arrived home one evening to find all your belongings packed in boxes. Your spouse announces, "Surprise! I've found a wonderful new house; we are moving tonight." We all need time to adjust to change. Take time to discuss the upcoming event with your child.

Some events you may wish to prepare your child for could include starting school or hospitalization. Whenever possible, arrange for your child to visit such settings in advance. Many of these places now have tours and programs designed specifically for this very purpose. Once you mention the event to your child, she may have many concerns and questions. Your availability and willingness to respond openly will help to alleviate her stress. As your child matures, you can begin to teach her skills for coping with stress. Chapter 9 has a section on helping your child learn self-calming skills.

Mindful Mommy
Reading a children's book about a similar topic can help your child prepare for a stressful event. He can identify with the characters and see what to expect. A positive conclusion to the story can be very reassuring.

Kids Benefit From Structure!

You can prevent many temper tantrums by adding structure. By adding structure to your child's schedule and environment, you can reduce many triggers for temper tantrums, including frustration, struggles for autonomy, insecurity, and fatigue.

Take a look at your child's physical environment, particularly the places where he spends a lot of time, such as his bedroom or playroom. Look for ways to make this a safe place for him to be independent and able to explore. Whenever possible, arrange toys and materials so they are accessible. You can also reduce your child's frustration by removing breakable and unsafe objects. This will minimize the times you will have to say no to your child and restrict him. By promoting your child's independence, you also build his confidence and self-control.

A child needs to have a sense of calm and order in her life. You can accomplish this by structuring her day. She will feel more in control when there are daily routines that follow a predictable pattern. She will learn what to expect, and she can begin to anticipate how to deal with it. A day without any predictable routine is very chaotic and disturbing to a young child. For example, it is midmorning and your toddler is playing in the yard. She is happily chasing butterflies when you call to her, "Okay, stop now and come with me." She freezes and looks at you, seemingly puzzled. You continue, "Let's go. I want you to take a nap now." Your demand is sure to meet with some resistance. If, on the other hand, you have a set routine for naptime at the same time each day, she will come to internalize your expectations and be more likely to comply.

Chapter 8

Triggers, Causes, and Explanations

YOU MAY HAVE HEARD that you should ignore your child's temper tantrums. That, after all, they are only fits that are staged either to manipulate you or to attract your attention. The truth is, many temper tantrums are a result of environmental, developmental, or maturity issues, and your child is not acting intentionally. So, no, your child is not trying to punish you!

However, as your child grows, she may learn that a temper tantrum and other behaviors such as whining are indeed effective ways to get what she wants. Let's take a closer look at specific types of tantrums. Call these triggers, causes, or explanations—soon you will have a much better understanding of what's going on in your little one's head!

Don't Go! Separation Tantrums

Despite your best efforts to prevent separation anxiety, it still is likely there will be times when you will contend with a crying and clinging child as you walk out the door. Separating from your young child may be just as stressful and heart-wrenching for you as it is for her. Be aware that your child will pick up on your apprehension and may feed off your negative emotions; if your body language is rigid and your voice sounds stern, it's not going to have a good effect. Resist negativity or implications that this should be an upsetting time. Some parents find that they are hurt when their child fails to show separation anxiety and tend to suggest directly or indirectly to the child that he should be upset. If your child is calm or unaffected by your preparation to leave, a statement like, "I know saying good-bye is scary, but don't cry" can be just the trigger to upset him—which is what you're trying to prevent in the first place.

The Mad Dash

If your child demonstrates true difficulty in saying good-bye, you may consider taking the easy way out, literally. It is tempting to avoid all the drama and tears and simply sneak out. This is a short-term fix and unadvisable. Leaving without saying good-bye is sneaky and can easily erode the feelings of trust you have worked so hard to establish. In the long run, your child will become more insecure and experience stronger anxiety if you sneak out.

Stand Your Ground

Because separations are often emotional and trying to both you and your child, you may easily find yourself swayed by your child's demands. Requests for "just one more kiss" or "five more minutes" are difficult to refuse. Again, in the long run, this often makes matters worse. You will find that good-byes will become easier if you stay the course and leave promptly after you say you will.

Of course, you want to be reassuring if your child is having a fit when it is time to say good-bye. Be firm and direct in explaining to your child what is happening. It may be helpful if your child has a clear sense of where you will be and what you will be doing while you are apart. You may even wish to show him your place of work or other setting so he can form a mental image of where you'll be. If your child is too young to understand time, use a concrete reference: "I'll be home after you eat lunch," or "When Sesame Street is over, you know it will be time for me to return."

Separation anxiety, as with other normal childhood behaviors, will fade over time. Be sure to recognize your child's progress and reassure her by helping her to remember that you always return when you say you will. As she matures, the assurance that you will remain a stable source of love and

Mindful Mommy

Establishing a routine adds predictability and a sense of security to separations. Maybe you can designate a special window for waving good-bye, or set a practice of just "two hugs and a kiss." One cute idea is to kiss the child's palm and close his fingers in. Explain to the child that now if he needs a kiss from you, he has one for later.

comfort, even when you are not there, will allow her to say good-bye with ease and rejoice when she sees you again.

It's All Mine! Possession Tantrums

Your young child will probably be resistant to sharing and may have sharing temper tantrums until she is five or six years old. It is important to realize that your child's emotional response is likely to be influenced by both her temperament and current mood. Although almost all young children have difficulty sharing, there are many different ways that your child may exhibit her anxiety or reluctance to share.

Walking Away

Your child has a friend over to visit for the afternoon. Your child is happily playing with her Legos at the kitchen table, and her friend is quietly watching her. You ask your child to share some of the Legos with her friend. Your child does not seem to become overly upset. However, instead of sharing, she puts her work back into the bin and leaves the table. This is her way of saying that she is not ready to share. It is okay to accept this response. Simply acknowledge her action by saying something like, "I can see that you chose to find a new activity rather than sharing the Legos. I am glad that you will let your friend have a turn, and I am sure you will rejoin her when you wish."

Wanting It Back

Your child has been pushing a toy car around the base of the tree. He then leaves it and starts to play with a dump truck instead. All is calm until his sister walks over and picks up the car. "Mine!" he screams. "I had that!" He still wants to play with the dump truck, but he wishes to maintain control over and a sense of ownership of the toy car. In the interest of fairness, you may explain to him that, if he wants another turn, then he will have to wait until his sister has had a turn.

If this seems to be a recurring problem for him, you can try to prevent it. When he appears to have stopped playing, you can ask him, "Are you sure that you are finished? If you stop playing with this toy, that means that you are ready to let someone else have a turn." There may still be times when he will change his mind, but this should help reduce the incidents.

Hoarding Toys

Sometimes, when your child is unwilling to release control of toys, she may hoard them. If she is hoarding toys, she is not really playing with them. You may see that she is simply collecting toys and holding on to as many as she can. Some children literally carry handfuls of toy pieces or cram toys into their pockets. Alternatively, she may be putting them in a hiding place or personal place to prevent other children from playing with them. You will need to intervene and help her make choices and then become involved with play. Try saying, "Let's find one toy that you can sit down and play with. You will have a chance to have a turn with one of the other toys after this activity."

Grabbing

Young children often grab toys away from other children. Egocentrism makes it hard for them to realize how their actions hurt the other child. You can bring this to their attention by saying something like, "When you grab the ball away from Lori, she feels sad. Can you see that she is crying? I'll bet you would be sad if someone grabbed a ball away from you."

Another reason that your young child is grabbing toys away from other children is that your child has a limited ability to communicate his needs or wants. With your guidance, he can learn to use words instead of grabbing. For example, you witness your child approach another child in the sandbox. He quickly reaches over and pulls a shovel away from the other child. You may say, "I can see that you wish to have a turn using that shovel. This child here was having a turn. You may not grab the shovel from her. If you want a turn, you need to use words. Now, let's return the shovel, and then you can ask for a turn."

Mommy Must

Remember, your child learns from your behavior as much as she does from your words. Avoid grabbing the toy away from her. You send her a mixed message if you grab a toy from her while you are telling her that grabbing is an unacceptable behavior.

If your child is very young, you may need to suggest words that he can use: "Let's ask this child, 'Can I have a turn?'"

Helping Your Child Share

If your child is in a situation in which she is having a hard time sharing, there are some things that you can do. First, if your child is having a full-blown tantrum over sharing, you will need to help her calm down. Your attempts at reasoning with her will be fruitless if she has lost emotional control. You will not be able to guide her through any conflict resolution when she is overwhelmed with feelings of anger or frustration.

When your child is having a hard time sharing a toy, you may find improvement if you use the term *turn taking* instead of sharing. The connotation is slightly different. Consider, if you share your ice cream, you lose part of it. Conversely, if you allow someone to have a turn with your blocks, the implication is that the blocks will be returned. Additionally, sharing may be tolerable if you can reassure your child that the item will be well cared for and that she, too, will have a turn.

Mommy Knows Best

Do not force your young child to share. Encouragement is fine, but coercion will only cause your child to feel anger and resentment. Ultimately, your child will learn to share for intrinsic reasons, such as a wish to make a friend happy.

When your child is in a battle with another child over a possession, there may be times when you will need to step in. You do not want to automatically solve all of your child's problems for her. Whenever possible, allow her and her friend to work through the conflict. She needs the direct hands-on experience of negotiation and resolving conflicts with her peers. There will be times, of course, that you may need to assist them.

Here are some guidelines for when to intervene during a sharing conflict:

- When either of the children seems emotionally out of control.
- When it is apparent that the conflict could escalate into violence.
- When the same conflict keeps recurring.
- When the children's resolutions continuously result in one of the children's being a victim or a loser.

When you do intervene, resist rushing in and making it all better immediately. Your role is to help the children by guiding them in the conflict-resolution process. Avoid asking the children, "Who had it first?" as this is bound to cause the children to blame or accuse each other, thereby only escalating the conflict. Start by clarifying or restating the problem: "Okay, it seems that both you and Joseph want to have a turn on the bicycle." Then you can prompt the children to explore potential solutions by asking them questions: "Can you think of a way that both of you can ride the bicycle?" "How can you find a fair answer so that you both will be satisfied?" "What can you do while Joseph is taking his turn?" Then guide them to follow through with their own solutions.

I'm a Big Kid Now!
Power Struggle Tantrums

By showing negativity or opposition to you, your child asserts his own awakening sense of power and control. The mantra for this stage is the word *no*. It may even seem that this has become your child's favorite word. It is often, literally, their declaration of independence. He has discovered that, when he uses the word no, he has the power to negate your guidance while expressing his own wishes or preferences. You may even discover that your child will say no to a suggestion that you know he actually wants to accept. You may offer a dream come true: "Would you like to go to Disneyland and eat pizza every day?" and he will still say no. To the extreme, some children will shift their wishes just to be in opposition to yours. For example, you say, "Okay, it is time to go inside." Your child says, "No!" "All right then, you can stay outside," you reply. However, your child answers, "No, I don't want to." When this happens, do not allow yourself to be drawn into an argument. If you can, give him a choice; if not, simply make a choice for him.

Your child may also choose to assert her power and control through nonverbal means. Nonverbal negativity behavior could include:

- Running from you when you tell him it is time to leave the playground.
- Going limp when you try to get her to walk into the doctor's office.
- Tensing his leg muscles and becoming rigid when you try to get him into the car seat.

There are some ways you can reduce your child's negativity. Be a good role model. Most parents do find they spend a lot of time restricting their toddler's behavior by using directives such as "no," "stop," or "don't." Try to reduce the number of times you have to say no to your child. You can do this by structuring his environment and removing hazards. When you do this, you provide freedom and safety for your child to explore. This will also foster her sense of autonomy. Try to state your expectations clearly: "Don't sit on the couch" can become "I need you to sit in your chair." Whenever possible, offer your child a choice. "Stop throwing sand" can become "You can use the

Mindful Mommy

You may feel strongly about your child telling you no. It is important to remember that, at this age, she is not being spiteful. She may be being disagreeable, but she is not being disrespectful.

sand to build either castles or roads, but you must keep the sand in the box."

The Power of Choice

Giving your child choices is a powerful way for you to eliminate much of your child's negativity and oppositional behavior. When your child has some choices, she has a sense of autonomy and power. Additionally, when your child makes a choice, then she has ownership of the choice she made and will be more likely to comply.

Consider carefully how much choice you are going to give your child. Choice is power. While giving your child some choices can be a valuable way to reduce power struggles in toddlers, you are not handing them the reins. Ultimately, you are still in control. There are many things that are not negotiable. When it comes to issues regarding your child's health and safety, for example, what you say goes. For example, you may allow your child to choose what color sweater she wants to wear or what brand of cereal she eats for breakfast. However, you do not let her choose whether to wear a sweater when it is cold or whether to eat a nutritious breakfast. Be sure to explain to your child, "I cannot offer you a choice about this. This is important for your health."

Real Choices

Do not give your child a choice unless there really is one available. You may inadvertently find yourself doing this by phrasing a request so that it sounds like a choice: "Wouldn't you like to come inside now?" or "Do you want to clean up your room, please?" When you give your child a choice, you must be prepared to honor his choice. Are you prepared for him to say no? This is also true even if your child chooses the option you did not anticipate. For example, "Either you can sit still at the circus or we are going home." If your child chooses to go home, then you need to follow through.

Limited Choices

Too many choices can be overwhelming for your child. Broad choices such as, "What do you want to eat for breakfast?" or "Where do you think we should go for the weekend?" do not help guide your child's behavior and may be hard for you to honor. What if your child asks for chocolate icing for breakfast or to go to Disneyworld for the weekend?

The key is to offer your child a limited choice. A limited choice gives your child two positive alternatives. Both alternatives are ones that you are prepared to accept. You have a predetermined expectation of how you want your child to behave, and you allow her to make choices within those parameters. For example, you want your child to eat a nutritious breakfast. You say, "Which do you want for break-fast—waffles or pancakes?" Of course, your toddler may still ask for chocolate icing. If this happens, remind her, "That is not one of your choices; you may choose either waffles or pancakes." There are many limited choices you can give your child each day. White socks or blue socks? Wheat bread or rye bread? Ponytail or braids?

When you give your child a limited choice, you help him:

- Comply with the behavior you want
- Feel independent and empowered
- Mitigate his urge for power struggles
- Understand expectations

The Illusion of Choice

There may be times when your young child is being oppositional over a behavior where there is no choice. Some parents find they can use a technique called the illusion of choice. Here, both choices you offer result in the same behavior that you want. However, the child is still permitted to feel some sense of power. For example, you want your child to take her allergy pill and she has clenched her jaw shut. The "choice" you give her may be, "You can take your pill with water or juice." The focus changes. The issue now is not whether she will take the pill, but the inconsequential choice of beverage.

Following Through

Along with the freedom of having a choice comes the responsibility to be accountable for the decision made. Not only should you honor your child's choice, but you need to be sure he does as well. You may find that your child sometimes has difficulty deciding and he wavers, and you will have to set a limit.

One mother shares, "Every choice I gave my daughter became a huge deal. I would ask if she wanted saltines or graham crackers for snack. Her typical response would be, 'Umm, saltines! No, graham crackers. No wait, saltines. Saltines, really saltines.' I would have the box out of the cabinet and she would throw a fit, crying for graham crackers." If your child has a hard time sticking with her choice, you may need to help her follow through. Advise your child to consider her choice carefully. Let her know that what she chooses is what she will get. Once she makes the choice, restate her choice as a conclusion: "Okay, you chose saltines. That is what you are going to have." If she balks at this, say, "This time you have chosen saltines. You may choose graham crackers next time."

At a Loss for Words: Emotional Tantrums

There are many possible causes for your child to behave aggressively. More often than not, he is lashing out. He is expressing his strong emotions the only way that he is able. Frustration and anger are

Mommy Must

Your preverbal child is probably not having a tantrum for attention or spite. Your role here is to calmly reassure her and help her regain control. Realize that it may take a while for her to settle down fully. Your patience will pay off.

expressed through hitting, biting, and other aggressive acts when the child is not able to say, "Stop that, you are making me angry!"

Here are some examples where lack of language may result in aggressive behavior, and possible ways to respond:

- She grabs a toy away from her younger sister. Say, "I can understand that you want a turn with the toy, but I need you to ask your sister for a turn."
- He shoves another child away while trying to get a seat at the table. Say, "It looks like you are trying to beat your friend to a seat. It is not safe to push. I will show you where you can sit."
- She kicks another child when that child knocked over her block tower. Say, "Boy are you upset! It is okay to be angry when someone wrecks your building, but I will not let you kick him."
- He throws a toy that does not seem to work. Say, "Are you mad that the toy won't go? Perhaps you can ask someone to help when things don't work."

Notice that each example response states the child's emotion or viewpoint. It is important that you recognize and accept your children's feelings. Everyone has the right to feel what he or she feels. You can show acceptance of your child's feelings without accepting his aggressive behavior. In other words, separate the deed from the doer. The underlying message is "I like you, but I don't like it when you ____." You can also see that each response clearly guides the child to a safer and more appropriate response to the child's problem. Your child's emotions have run out of control and turned into a full-scale tantrum; you need to help her put the brakes on her emotions before you can deal with any other issues.

Crying, screaming, and aggression are hard to stop midstream, but here are different strategies you can try to help your child calm down:

- Remain calm. Respond with a calm and quiet voice. If you are emotional or raise your voice, you are likely to fuel the fire.
- Show empathy. Communicate that you are right there and listening: "I know you are feeling ____. I am here to help you."
- Change the venue. Remove your child from a situation or person that is upsetting him. Also, there may be times when you can distract him with humor or a toy.
- Use the power of touch. Try stroking her hair or rubbing his back. Some parents find that they need to hold their child close to help her feel calm and secure.

The Truth about Biting

One of the most troublesome behaviors, from a parent's perspective, is biting. Yet biting is a very common behavior from the time children start teething, through their toddler years.

But Why?

In order to control a behavior, you first need to understand why it occurs. Many young children bite when they are overwhelmed with feelings of anger or frustration. This is most likely to be true if your child is impulsive and has yet to learn how to express herself verbally. Biting is a very powerful way to release strong feelings.

Your child may begin teething at four to seven months of age. When her gums are swollen, she may discover that biting can relieve feelings of discomfort and pain.

Children younger than age two or three rely on direct hands-on sensory experiences to form concepts and understanding. This means that they are learning about something if they can see, hear, touch, and so forth. When your child bites you, he may simply be trying to discover, "What will it feel like to bite Mom? How will she taste? How will she react?" Biting usually diminishes once the child acquires verbal skills.

How to Respond to Biting

If you observe your child carefully, you may be able to determine when he is likely to bite. Perhaps it is when he is tired or over-stimulated. You can then be proactive. Provide your child with that much-needed nap or remove him from the circumstances.

You will also know when it is wise to keep an extra eye on him and be available to intervene.

If you suspect teething is the problem, be sure to provide your child with a cool teether or rubber ring. Some parents will attach one to their child's clothing so it is always handy. When your child begins to bite someone, stop him and explain, "Biting hurts people. If you need to bite, use your teething ring. Teething rings are for biting."

Help your child learn consequences and see how their behavior affects someone else. Again, as you stop him from biting, say, "Biting hurts people." You can show him that the victim is crying or that there is a mark on the victim's skin. If the victim is able, ask him to tell the biter that he is hurt. Focus attention on caring for the child who has been bitten. Ask your child to participate in helping the victim feel better. Maybe he can get a Band-Aid or ice or simply offer a hug to the hurt child. Biting, along with other aggressive behaviors, will likely decrease once your child has acquired the adequate language skills he needs to express his emotions and solve his own problems with words.

Mommy Knows Best

You may have been told to bite your child when your child bites someone. Resist this reaction—it will backfire. Rather than teaching your child that biting hurts, you are sending the message that it is okay to bite someone if she bites you first or if you are angry.

Look at Me! Attention Tantrums

When it comes to attention temper tantrums, your response will have a tremendous impact. In fact, your responses will either squelch or fuel your child's attention temper tantrums. Your child needs to learn that temper tantrums will not get her what she wishes, and that she will need to adopt appropriate behavior.

Stand Your Ground

You may be determined to stand your ground, but there are times when your resolve may waver. You may be particularly challenged when you are tired, frustrated, stressed, or feeling guilty. Unfortunately, once you give in, all of the other times that you did not will be forgotten by your child. Consistency is crucial.

There are many reasons why you should not give in. First and foremost, you are rewarding your child for having a tantrum. When you give in, you give up power and authority. This may be upsetting to the child who counts on you for boundaries and guidance. You are not helping your child learn. When you give in, you take away the opportunity for your child to learn to manage her frustration independently. Sooner or later, you will not be there to provide what your child wants or to jump in to solve her problem. It may sound harsh, but your child does need to have experience in not getting her own way so she knows how to deal with it.

Choose Your Words Carefully

Briefly acknowledge your child when she is clearly throwing an attention temper tantrum. Show that you understand what she is feeling as you set the limit: "I know that you want a cookie, but it is too close to dinnertime." "I can see that you are mad, but you have to stay with Grandma today."

Clearly inform your child what the consequences will be. Let him know that he will not get what he wants and you will not continue to respond to his behavior. Do not allow your child to pull you into an argument. If he keeps whining or insisting, "But why? Oh, please!" simply restate your expectations. "I will not discuss this with you until you are calm." End the conversation by saying, "Let me know when you are done having a temper tantrum. Let me know when you are ready to be calm."

How to Respond Reasonably

Ensure that your child is safe. Clear away any hazards if she is thrashing about. You may need to stand close by to keep her safe and to let her know that you will be available when the temper tantrum is over. Next, stop responding to her behavior. Do

Mindful Mommy

Be on guard for times when you may be more likely to give in. Is your resolve shaken when your child is whining or screaming? Is mealtime or bedtime particularly trying? Perhaps you are more likely to give in when the temper tantrum occurs in public or you are worried that other people are judging your parenting ability.

your best to ignore her. Yes, this may be difficult. At first, her demands may escalate as she tries to get a reaction from you. Stand your ground. Do not speak to her, touch her, or look directly at her. Some parents will pretend to be engaged in other activities, such as listening to music, reading, or folding laundry. One mother shares:

> *My son would have horrible tantrums. He would kick and scream and my insides would churn, ready to explode. One day, I found my husband's earplugs from work. I put them in; it was heaven. I could see my son and know that he was okay but the sound didn't drive me batty. I love it. Whenever I feel like I can't cope with the sound of a tantrum, I hunt down the earplugs. What I have learned is that my lack of reaction usually results in the tantrum's diminishing.*

Eventually, your child will recognize that the tantrum is not producing the results that he was hoping for and he will stop. When he indicates that he is calm and in control, you can respond to him once again. Treat the end of a temper tantrum very

Mommy Must

You may be able to respond calmly with your child when he is having a temper tantrum that is caused by temperament or developmental growth. However, you may not find it as easy to be patient when you feel that he is intentionally staging a tantrum for attention or to manipulate you in some way. It is still important that you keep your composure and remain objective.

matter-of-factly. Resist the temptation to lecture, warn, or moralize. If you make a big fuss now, you may still inadvertently reinforce his temper tantrum.

It's Too Hard! Frustration Tantrums

As your child is developing and trying to master many new skills, there will surely be times when they are frustrated. By the way that you respond to your child when she is frustrated, you can help her cope with her strong feelings. You also have the opportunity to help her learn how to manage her frustration in the future. To effectively respond to your child's frustration, you need to be alert and in tune with her threshold for frustration. Each child is different. Some remain calm and persistent when challenged, and other children try something only once before becoming overwhelmed. By careful observation, you may also learn specific triggers for your child's frustration. Does he tend to become more frustrated when he is being evaluated? Does competition make him feel stress, and therefore make him less resilient to frustration? Additionally, consider if your child is more frustrated by certain tasks. Perhaps she can calmly tackle her math home-work but she falls to pieces if she is trying to master a new dance step. Knowing your child's threshold and triggers will help you prevent some frustration for her and will help you respond with sensitivity when she is having difficulties.

Empathy is Key!

The most powerful thing you can do when your child is frustrated is to respond with empathy. Let your child know you hear and understand what he is feeling. You can be specific and show that you empathize by saying things such as, "Look at all those pieces! I can understand why this puzzle is driving you bonkers." Or, "I know this homework is challenging your ability to stay calm."

Responding with empathy helps to diffuse your child's strong feelings of aggravation or frustration. You show him that his feelings are acceptable and understandable. You are helping him gain the perspective that he is not alone in feeling this way. The knowledge that someone else can relate to this experience, and that it is okay to feel frustrated, because everyone gets frustrated at times, will be effective in helping your child manage his frustration.

Encouragement *Will* Help

Your response should be encouraging. Encouraging statements will help your child stay positive about tackling the current task. Encouraging statements also build your child's confidence, something she will

Mommy Knows Best

With experience, you will learn when to intervene or respond when your child is frustrated. You may find that by responding quickly, you can prevent your child's frustrations from escalating. Alternatively, you may find that if you jump in too rapidly, your child may be resentful and resistant to your help. A good rule of thumb: the younger the child, the quicker your response should be.

need to be successful in the future. You can encourage your child by saying things like, "I have faith that you will be able to do it. I am confident you can find the answer." Or, "Your hard work will pay off."

When children (and adults) are frustrated, they often send themselves discouraging messages and develop their own internal negative voice. That voice sends messages such as, "This is too hard for me," "If I were not so dumb, I could do this," "I bet I will just fail again." If you continue to encourage your child, you will replace those negative messages with positive ones such as, "I know I can," and "I bet I will find the answer."

Preventing Frustration Tantrums

Although you cannot prevent all frustration temper tantrums, there are steps you can take to reduce them. To keep your young child safe, it's necessary to put restrictions on some of their activities and behavior. Toddlers struggling with their own autonomy will often feel frustrated with so many limits. Many times during a day, the typical toddler hears, "Stop doing that" or "Don't touch that." Whenever possible, provide your child with a place where they can safely play and explore with few limits. You can keep those necessary limits and reduce your child's frustration simply by limiting negative statements and putting a positive spin on your directives. Change those negative messages to, "I need you to put that down and come sit with me" and "You can play with this toy instead."

Set up your child for success, not failure. Look at your expectations for your child. Are they both age appropriate and on target for his capabilities? He will base his own sense of accomplishment and competence on how he perceives he measures up to your expectations. Avoid crafts that have a set pattern or model. Stay away from kits or paint-by-numbers sets. If you do crafts or projects with her, emphasize the process rather than the finished result. Instead of having her glue cutout shapes to make a kitty picture that looks like one in the craft book, why not give her a variety of supplies and encourage her to explore and create what she wishes? Some good examples of materials that focus on process rather than product include clay, finger paints, collage materials, and papier-mâché.

It is okay to have positive expectations for your child. However, when she is young, focus on her effort and personal improvement rather than on her achievements. For example, "I can see how hard you are tying to snap your jacket" or "I see you are spending more time practicing your piano lessons." What counts here is not her accomplishment or skill but her effort. With your encouragement, she will keep trying.

Mindful Mommy

Are you sending your child unintended messages that she does not or will never measure up to? Stop yourself before you say things like, "Why can't you be more like your big brother?" "I was always good at math, so what is your problem?" or "I'll be so embarrassed if you do not make the team."

Chapter 9

Teach Your Child Skills for Coping

ARE YOU FINDING THAT your six-year-old daughter still has many temper tantrums and episodes when she loses control? Think she should be "over it" by now? Is she very compliant and quick to calm down and respond to your guidance? Can you easily help her solve problems and manage the crisis, when you're there? But the problem is, when you are not around, she can-not control her own behavior? You know you will not be able to hover over her every waking moment. What can you do?

Helping Your Child with Self-Control

Much of parenting is about connecting with your child and guiding your child's behavior. You must intervene to stop or redirect your child when his behavior is inappropriate or unsafe, much as a police officer would. Children without self-control may behave appropriately in your presence but continue to act out or sneak things when you are not there. Of course, you cannot always be there; eventually your child needs to make independent choices and control her own behavior. This is the goal of self-control, to internalize rules and standards of behavior.

There are many skills for your child to master to learn self-control. In many cases, you can provide experiences of direct instruction to promote self-control. You do not have to wait for opportunities to occur naturally.

Less Lashing-Out Incidents

Becoming less impulsive is a big part of self-control. Children naturally react to situations impulsively. When distressed or angered, they are inclined to lash out emotionally. An impulsive child acts first and thinks later. In other words, she looks before she leaps.

The goal is for your child to pause and recognize how she feels and wishes to act. Then she needs to evaluate the possible consequences of the behavioral choices she could make. She needs to foresee, "If I ___, then ___ will happen." For example, "If I leave my socks on the porch, then they will get wet and muddy." At first, getting your child to stop while she is preparing to act is tricky. It is best when you can catch your child at this moment. For example, your child has been arguing with a playmate and now you see him swinging a large block near his friend's head. Stop your child when you see he is acting impulsively. Do this with physical contact or even a signal such as a whistle or clearing your throat. Some parents are able to master "the look." They make eye contact with their child and show a facial expression that, without any words, says, "Stop now, and I mean business!" Next, directly ask your child what he had planned to do next. Some children will be shocked to realize that they were about to hurt someone. They were reacting but not thinking. You then want to help him evaluate the consequences of his intended action: "What will happen if you hit Vinny? How will he feel? Is this really what you want to do?"

You can help your child learn to stop and evaluate her impulses before she acts by having her imagine a big Stop sign when she feels angry or frustrated. You can help your child learn this control by teaching her games that give her practice in literally stopping her intentions. Here are two suggested games that you may recall from your own childhood.

Red Light/Green Light

Any number of children can play. All children line up side by side. One child is chosen to be the "traffic cop." He goes and stands fifty feet or so in front of the group, and then he turns his back. The traffic cop chants, "Red light, green light, go!" When the traffic cop says "go," the children in the line are to begin running toward the traffic cop. After a few seconds, the traffic cop says, "Red light, green light, stop!" and all the children must stop and freeze very quickly. When the traffic cop says, "stop," he also turns around to face the other players. If the traffic cop spots any of the players moving, they must go back to the starting line. The traffic cop will repeat this pattern of commands in rapid succession. The first player to reach the traffic cop becomes the new traffic cop, and all of the other children return to the starting line.

Statues

There are two versions of this game. In the first version, music is played for the children to dance to; when the music stops, all the children must freeze and hold the position they were in while they were dancing. When a child is caught moving, she is eliminated. The second version is a bit more involved. One person plays the role of an art dealer. This person takes each player by the hands and gently spins them around. When they let go, the player must strike a pose. A second child comes in to look at the statues. He will choose (buy) only a statue that is not moving. The last statue bought becomes the new art dealer or customer.

Mommy Knows Best

The ability to become less impulsive and to stop and evaluate the consequences of one's behavior has long-lasting benefits. It will help your child manage frustration and improve her social skills while she is young. Having the ability to evaluate choices will help her later in life to resist peer pressure to engage in risk-taking behaviors such as drug use or gang involvement.

Remembering Rules

A useful technique for helping your child develop self-control is called prompting. When you use prompting, you are stopping your child when you are displeased with his behavior, and asking him to evaluate his actions. Rather than simply reminding your child of a rule or guideline, you are asking him to recall the rule and implications. For example, "What is the rule about hitting?" "What should you do when you are mad at your sister?" "What happens when you leave your toys on the stairs?" Remember to keep your list of rules short and simple. Your young child will genuinely need to be reminded of a rule many times before she will fully internalize it and abide by it. Prompting is an effective way to help your child internalize rules and standards of behavior. Ultimately, your voice of guidance becomes the "little voice" in your child's head.

Thinking Ahead

Once your child has learned to stop his impulsive behavior midstream, he is ready to make purposeful choices about his behavior. He is learning to remember rules and predict consequences. Once your

Mindful Mommy

Young children have a very limited memory capacity. Before your child is four or five years old, you will need to remind her of the rules, directly and with prompting, many times. When you find yourself saying, "How many times do I have to tell you to ___?" try to stay patient and realize that your child is not intentionally forgetting.

157

child can predict the consequences of a behavior, he will be more able to control his behavior. This will allow your child to plan his response for any given situation.

Established routines help your child think ahead. Remind your child of routines and set expectations. Slowly you can encourage your child to take some control of routines. Prompting can be very helpful in assisting your child to make appropriate choices within a routine: "What else should you do to get ready for bed?" "What is the first thing you should do when you get home from school? What comes next?"

Surviving the Storm

Just like you, your child is bound to experience strong feelings on occasion. When your child is young, his emotions are very close to the surface and may change rapidly; this can be very overwhelming for him. Some feelings that a young child may have difficulty handling include disappointment, frustration, and anger. Angry feelings range from mild irritation to intense rage. It is important to note that strong feelings often include physiological responses such as a rapid heart rate, muscle tension, or accelerated breathing. These reactions will add to your child's perception of being overwhelmed or out of control.

Talk About Feelings

Having feelings is a hallmark of being human. It is important that you allow and accept all of your child's emotions. On the other hand, you do not have to allow or accept her actions. For example, you might say, "I understand that you are feeling angry, but I cannot permit you to bite Lynda. That is not safe." "It is okay that you feel tired and cranky, but it is not okay for you to throw your food across the room."

Respect your child's feelings and you will help him learn to express and control them appropriately. Avoid discounting your child's emotions. What he is feeling is very real and important to him. You may recall a time when someone patted you on the head and told you, "Don't worry your pretty little head" or "Don't be silly; you should not be so upset." More than likely, you found that a condescending or dismissive response would only flame your already heated emotions. Your child has the right to feel whatever she truly feels. Helping her express that feeling is where you play a part.

Mindful Mommy

It is tempting to encourage your child to suppress his strong emotions. "Big boys don't cry" is a common adage. We now know this is not good advice. Suppressing emotions does not make them go away. With no safe outlet, bottled-up emotions often are to blame for many adult ailments, everything from headaches to ulcers to heart disease.

Help Your Child Identify Emotions

A child as young as two years old can start to learn skills for controlling and expressing strong emotions. The first step is for her to be able to identify and label what she is feeling. From the start, make a point of recognizing and labeling your child's feelings for her by saying something like, "Oh, I see you are stomping your feet. I think you are feeling angry." You can prompt your preschooler to identify what emotion she is experiencing: "Trudy, I saw you push Sam. What feeling made you act this way?"

Your child can learn more about her own emotions if you guide her in identifying the emotions of other people. There are specific activities to help your child learn this skill:

- Create flashcards using pictures of people with various facial expressions. Ask your child to label what each person is feeling.
- Use magazine pictures for a project. Ask your child to make a collage of people who look sad, angry, or happy.
- Share a favorite book or movie with your child. Ask her to analyze what a character may be feeling. How did Cinderella feel when she had to stay home from the ball? What do you think Peter Rabbit felt when he was caught in Mr. McGregor's garden?
- Continue the discussion of the story's character by asking your child how she knows how the character is feeling. For example, you

might say, "Look at Cinderella's face. How do you think she feels? How can you tell that she feels that way? How would you feel if you had to stay home from the ball?"

Expressing Emotion

As your child matures, you can teach him specific ways to express his emotions. Your focus is to help your child use words to express how he is feeling. Helping your child with verbal expression will give him a sense of control and reduce emotional outbursts and tantrums.

It is also helpful to provide physical outlets for your child. A few ways your child can use her body to express emotions are exercising, dancing, drawing "angry" pictures, or going for a walk.

Teaching Problem Solving 101

Solving problems is an important skill. Both children and adults meet with problems or conflict almost every day. Some problems your child may face will be small, such as trying to get shoes to fit on a doll.

Mommy Knows Best

Recent studies show that preschool-aged children who cannot read and interpret the facial expressions of other children will be more likely to be aggressive once they enter school. There is an early connection between emotional understanding and behavioral problems.

Other problems your child may encounter, such as how to handle a bully, are more complex. If your child learns to solve problems while he is young, he will have a greater sense of control and a higher tolerance for frustration.

You Are a Role Model

Your child will learn a lot about problem solving by observing you. Imitation is a powerful way to learn. If your child witnesses you calmly and methodically following the steps above, she will be more likely to handle problems the same way.

Consider the following scenario. You and your child have just returned home from a long afternoon of shopping. On the doorstep, you balance your packages as your dig through your purse or pockets for the house key. Your key is gone! Do you lose emotional control and start crying and cursing as your frantically dump out everything onto the porch? Alternatively, do you model appropriate coping and problem-solving skills, sometimes involving your child in the process? For example, you might say, "Oh, dear, the key is lost and we are locked out of the house. Can you help me think of another way to get

Mommy Knows Best

Regardless of the problem, first, you must correctly identify the problem or the underlying issue. The second step is to brainstorm possible solutions. Next, you evaluate alternatives and possible consequences. Last, you pick a solution to try. If the choice works, you adopt this behavior for similar problems. If the solution does not work, you will try another.

in? Hmmm, the garage door is locked, too. I need to think of someone else who has a key."

Responsible Response

How you respond when your child has a problem will influence her future problem-solving skills. Imagine that you see that your four-year-old is struggling with a jigsaw puzzle. She is becoming increasingly frustrated with a particular piece and is now on the verge of tears. There are four basic response styles—which is yours?

Sensitive. You say, "Aww, I see you are really upset. Why don't we play with another toy?" This response may make your child feel better but will not help her learn the new skill or how to manage future frustration.

Critical. You say, "Stop crying over that silly puzzle. It is clear that it is too difficult for you." The critical response will only frustrate your child further and will cause her to doubt her own ability or competence.

Fixing. You say, "Oh, look, the red piece needs to . . . never mind, I will finish it for you." This type of response will eliminate the frustration but will only increase your child's dependence on you.

Coaching. You say, "I can see how frustrated you are becoming. What shape do you think you need?

What direction can you try with that piece?" The coaching response will encourage your child to manage frustrations and become an independent problem solver.

Avoid the temptation to intervene right away; give your child the opportunity to solve the problem on his own. Sometimes, you can give him a nudge with questions such as, "Do you have an idea?" or "What do you think would happen if you ____?" This is the time to brainstorm. Explore even silly or far-fetched ideas. Remember that practice will improve your child's skills.

Different Ages, Different Abilities

Even infants and toddlers are beginning to learn how to solve problems. They are learning by direct hands-on exploration. Learning at this age comes from doing, by trial and error. Slowly, your child can see the consequences of his actions. You can see this as he tries to get a round shape into a square hole or a block to balance on its end. By making mistakes, he discovers how to alter his behavior to achieve an intended result. Give your infant or toddler plenty

Mommy Must

Select toys that your child can explore and manipulate to see cause and effect. Some toys good for this are stacking rings, rattles, spinning toys, See 'n Say, or a jack-in-the-box. Toys that can be played with in more than one way, like boxes and blocks, are ideal.

of toys and materials for play and experimentation. Guide him in resolving simple problems such as retrieving a toy that is out of reach.

As your child ages, her ability to master problem solving will improve. Advancing verbal skills will aid her negotiation ability. Improved memory capacity will help her recall consequences of her behavior and will aid in learning through imitation. Now your child can try out multiple solutions and compare their effectiveness.

Role-playing is a great way to teach your child how to work through different alternatives. You can engage your preschooler's imagination by using dolls or puppets. Set up a scenario of interest with your child. Play "Let's pretend." Here are some suggestions for possible conflicts: Mr. Frog grabs the block away from Miss Spider, both Piglet and Pooh want the honey pot first, or three bears find two apples in the forest. Be sure to include a discussion of each of the points of view and of the possible feelings of the characters. Remember to involve your child in generating possible solutions. Encourage your child to script the action. For example, you can ask her, "What can Miss Spider say to Mr. Frog so that she can get the block returned to her?"

Your school-aged child is starting to understand abstract thought. This frees him from trial-and-error learning. He does not have to physically try out multiple solutions; now he can imagine hypothetical situations and outcomes. Help your child develop these skills and learn to analyze and evaluate alternative solutions with the following activities:

Use storybooks as a springboard for a discussion. Identify problems that characters are facing and evaluate how their problems are resolved.

At the top of a large piece of butcher paper, list a potential problem or conflict the child has already experienced. Below, make two columns and title them "Good Choice" and "Bad Choice." Write potential reactions to the problem on index cards and have your child decide where each card belongs. Here is an example problem: You want the puppet that Jimmy is playing with. Here are example reactions: (a) You snatch the toy away from Jimmy, (b) You ask Jimmy for a turn, (c) You find a new toy to play with until Jimmy is done, and (d) You bring a new puppet and ask Jimmy if he wishes to trade.

Cooling Down Cues

The ability to develop skills for self-soothing and self-calming is important. Children and adults who have these skills handle stress and frustration better than those who don't. You can promote in your child the ability to maintain emotional equilibrium and to roll with the punches. There are strategies appropriate for all ages.

Soothing Young Children

Many young infants and toddlers adopt their own self-soothing behaviors. Thumb sucking may be the earliest example, but other children may rock gently, rub their face with a blanket or other loved object, or twirl their hair. There are many ways you can try to calm your child. Try some of the following to find which works best for your child:

- Play soft music.
- Provide white or droning noise (such as a vacuum).
- Rock your child.
- Stroke or massage your child.

As your child approaches toddlerhood, there are some fun activities that you can use to show your child how to calm herself down. Show her how to relax her body. Ask your child to let her muscles go limp and pretend to be a rag doll. Alternatively, ask her to swirl and twirl scarves in the air. Ask your young child to move like an animal: Stomp through mud like an elephant, fly and glide like a bird, and so forth. These activities force your child to slow down, relax, and move in a calm, controlled manner.

Activities that involve the sense of touch (kinesthetic activities) are often very soothing for young children. Use a bucket or dishpan for a sensory activity. Fill the bucket with water or sand or shaving cream or any tactile material your child may enjoy.

Play dough, Gak, Silly Putty, and clay also are very calming materials for your child to manipulate.

Older Children, Different Abilities

As your child matures, his ability to calm himself down will improve. Adults as well as children can use many of the activities below. Introduce your child to a variety of strategies and let him discover what works best for him.

Help your child find a special "get away from it all" place. This can be a quiet room in the cellar, a grassy spot under an apple tree, or even just a comfy chair. Any place that he can call his own and where he will be undisturbed will work.

Provide opportunities for your child's self-expression. A journal or sketchpad can sometimes help your child vent in a safe way. Provide him with any materials he may need, such as pencils, crayons, and so forth. Be sure to reassure your child that his journal is a private thing for him and that you will not look at it unless he invites you to.

Show your child ways to relax her body with these exercises. Sit quietly, take deep breaths through

Mommy Knows Best

Play dough recipe: Mix 1/2 cup salt and 1 cup flour together. Add 1 cup water, 1 tablespoon cooking oil, and 1 tablespoon cream of tartar. Heat over low heat and stir. When it clumps up, remove mixture from heat and knead in a few drops of food coloring. Store in an airtight container.

your nose, and exhale slowly. Try imagining you are breathing through your feet. Listen to the sound of your breath. Curl your body into a tight ball. Slowly uncoil yourself like a cat stretching out. Be sure to slowly stretch as far as you can go. Close your eyes. Focus on one part of your body; clench it tightly. Then relax that part slowly. Imagine it is very loose and heavy. Work from your head to your toes.

Guide your child with creative visualization. You can read or tape scripts for your child to listen to. Here are three to try.

Light as a Feather

Close your eyes and relax. Imagine you are a light little feather. You are dropping slowly from a big white fluffy cloud in the sky. Feel yourself softly sway back and forth. Feel how the wind is pushing you as you glide downward. You are swaying back and forth, back and forth, and back and forth. Feel how a cool breeze makes you tumble through the air. You are slowly descending until you come to a gentle stop on the ground.

Mindful Mommy

Along with general relaxation, these techniques may result in many other benefits to both adults and children, including improved concentration, memory, and creativity. Some report that such relaxation techniques improve their sleep and general well-being as well.

At the Beach

You are lying on the warm sand at the beach. You can feel the cool and gritty sand under your back. You feel your feet sinking a bit in the moist sand. You now notice how warm the sun feels on your skin. When you turn your head, you can see all of the tiny crystals of sand, glimmering like diamonds in the sunlight. Take a deep breath; you can smell the warm, salty sea air and the lingering fragrance of suntan lotion. In the distance, you can hear children playing, a gull crying, and the waves crashing on the shore.

In the Forest

You are sitting underneath a great big tree in the middle of the forest. You are resting your back on the hard, rough, and knobby trunk of the tree. You can feel cool spongy moss under your hands as you rest them on the ground. At your feet is a babbling brook. The cool water is splashing up against the rocks and a refreshing spray is hitting your legs. The sunlight is streaming though the leaves and creating a dappled pattern on the forest floor. You close your eyes and you can hear the wind rustling through the leaves and the call of an unknown bird.

Chapter 10

Struggling to Keep the Peace

So WE ALL KNOW by now that temper tantrums are a normal occurrence of childhood. Although some of your child's temper tantrums may be very intense, you will find that they will resolve quickly—thank Goodness! On rare occasions, you may find that your child has lost complete control of her emotions and behavior and you will need to help her reign them in. How do you cope when all of your past tried-and-true calming strategies are not working?

Escalating Out of Control?

Most temper tantrums are like summer storms: They arrive with a lot of flash and noise, but they pass fairly quickly. On rare occasions, you may find that your child's temper tantrum is not subsiding as you would expect it to. In fact, it's becoming more intense with each passing moment. Nothing you say or do seems to work, as your child's tantrum continues to escalate.

Strong Feelings, Strong Response

Toddlers are the most likely to have temper tantrums that escalate. This is because they have very little ability to understand or control their own emotions. Consequently, your child may become overwhelmed or frightened by his strong feelings. Additionally, once in the throes of a temper tantrum, the feeling of being out of control can be very upsetting. You may discover that your child's tantrum has become his response to feeling out of control and that he has forgotten what triggered his temper tantrum in the first place. Some children will get so worked up that they will urinate or vomit while they are having a temper tantrum. Avoid punishing your child if this happens. It is unintentional. Not only has he lost emotional control, but he has also lost physical control.

Gaining Back Control

You may have to alter the way that you would normally respond to your child's temper tantrum in this situation. Here are some guidelines. Stay calm. Your child is counting on you to help her regain control. No matter how heated your child's temper becomes, use a calm voice and gentle actions.

Keep her safe. If your child is out of control and thrashing about, you need to take action to prevent her from hurting herself or others. You may even have to pick up your child and move her to a safer place.

Stand back. If your child is completely hysterical, your attempts to distract or calm her may be futile. Your child may be too overwhelmed to listen or think rationally. Wait until after the storm has passed before you attempt to talk about the temper tantrum.

Holding Your Child Close

There may be times when your child is so out of control that you will need to take dramatic action to keep him safe and secure. When your child is a threat to himself or people nearby, and nothing else works, you can try a "hug hold." Use this technique only as a last resort, and only when you feel calm and in control of your own emotions.

Perform a hug hold gently but firmly.

1. Sit behind your child and cross your legs over your child's legs.
2. Reach around the front of your child and hold his arms across his body. Simply let your child know that you are holding him until he is ready to be safe and in control.
3. Hold your child until you feel he has achieved some calm and self-control.

Mindful Mommy

Sometimes you can stop the trend of rising emotional distress if you can break through your child's hysteria and get his attention. Try flashing the lights off and on, whispering in his ear, or making funny noises.

Let's take a look at a real-life example, maybe you can relate! One mother recalls:

I only had to restrain my son once. He was playing in the cellar with two of his friends from down the street. I don't know what started the incident. All of a sudden, I heard a ruckus and ran down the steps. My son was yelling at his friends about something being unfair. He had taken off his cowboy boots and was trying to hit one of his friends with them. I went over and took his boots away and put them on a shelf. I then tried to sit him down to talk with him. He was so totally out of control that he jumped back and pushed over the chair. He ran over to the shelf, grabbed his boots, and threw them at his friend. He then started to take other things off the shelf and began throwing them. I managed to get behind him and hold on to him. I sat in a chair while I put my legs and arms around him. He was furious. He began screaming at me, "Let me go! Argggh! Let me free!" I tried the best that I could to stay calm and told him that I would hold him until he was in control. He tried to buck back and forth and he tried to spit on my arms! I repeatedly told him that I would hold him safe until he was ready to be in control. Finally, I could feel his body relax and he started to cry. I loosened my hold but still held him until he fully settled down.

Understanding Aggression

Understanding why your child may be aggressive toward others may be difficult. The bottom line is that hurting other people is your child's response to anger or frustration. This is your child's way of expressing these strong emotions. Each child is different; some children are more likely to lash out than others are. There are many factors that may influence your child's aggressive behavior.

Aggression Breeds Aggression

Your child's environment and early experiences will have an impact on her tendency to be aggressive. Research shows that, when young children are exposed to violence or aggression, they are more likely to be aggressive themselves. Your child may be exposed to violence and aggression because she is growing up in a high-crime or war-torn neighborhood. Violence may be close to home and have a stronger impact. In homes where a child is a witness to domestic violence, she observes aggression as a model for emotional expression and conflict resolution.

Mindful Mommy

Children are very vulnerable, and direct exposure to violence can have a lasting impact. One study found that, if children are first exposed to violence before the age of eleven, they will be three times more likely to develop psychiatric problems than children who are exposed later in life.

Direct exposure to violence affects children differently depending on their age. When young children are exposed to violence, they tend to respond in a more passive way. They may become clingier and show more problems with separation anxiety. They may become generally more fearful and anxious and develop a fear of abandonment. As a result, they may have more nightmares. A younger child may also regress in her behavior and start sucking her thumb or wetting her bed again.

Young children will sometimes act out themes of aggression and violence in their play. By role-playing, they can safely examine and explore their fears while still being in control.

When school-aged children are directly exposed to violence, it will usually affect their behavior. They may become more aggressive and destructive. Alternatively, you may see them become withdrawn and depressed. They will often have difficulty at school as they have problems concentrating. School-aged children may also complain of physical problems such as headaches and stomachaches, and they may become depressed.

Mommy Knows Best

If you use spanking or any form of physical punishment, your child is more likely to be physically aggressive. This is true even if you are punishing him for aggressive behavior in the first place. To your child, your actions are more influential than your words are, and they send the message, "Do as I do, not as I say."

Different Types of
Aggressive Behavior

There are three main types of aggressive behavior: displaced aggression, instrumental aggression, and hostile aggression. Displaced aggression is when your child's behavior is not directed at the person or object who has angered or frustrated her. This most commonly occurs when your child realizes that she cannot behave aggressively toward the cause of her strong feelings. Perhaps she knows that it would be socially unacceptable, or perhaps she knows that she will get in trouble for doing so. As a result, she takes out her anger or frustration on a safe and more acceptable target. Let's consider an example, you may see this if Dad has told your child that it's time for her to stop playing and get ready for bed. She is angry and frustrated with Dad, but she knows that she cannot yell back at him. She enters the house crying and whining, then kicks the dog.

Using aggression as a means to a goal is called instrumental aggression. For example, your child may push someone out of the way to get a seat closer to the television. Instrumental aggression will decrease as your child matures and becomes less impulsive. Hostile aggression, on the other hand, tends to occur more frequently with older children. Hostile aggression is when your child intentionally sets out to harm someone else. Children who are most likely to use hostile aggression tend to have or mistrustful demeanor and outlook. They tend to lash out in either self-defense or retaliation at those who they perceive (realistically or not) will or have hurt them.

Television Plays a Part

There is no longer any doubt: Countless research studies have shown that violent content on TV influences a child's aggressive behavior. The impact is greater on children with emotional, behavioral, or impulse-control problems. Additionally, children are more likely to imitate the behaviors in shows in which the violence is particularly realistic or in which the aggressor goes unpunished or is rewarded. It does not seem to matter if the show is animated or live action.

In addition to leading him to imitate what he sees, viewing violent and aggressive acts on TV can have other effects on your child. Studies show that the child who views violent programming may begin to accept aggression as a way to solve problems. He will also become desensitized to acts of violence and

Mindful Mommy

Children spend an average of twenty-three hours a week watching TV. The average child will spend more time watching TV than he will spend in school. Guidelines from the American Academy of Pediatrics recommend that children under the age of two should not watch TV at all, and older children should be limited to less than two hours a day.

aggression. These children will display an increased level of fearfulness and mistrust.

Realistically, it is probably not feasible or even desirable to completely ban your child from watching television. Therefore, it is wise for you to monitor closely and limit what your child watches on TV. Take advantage of TV program rating guides or the V chip. Whenever possible, work with your child to discuss and plan appropriate viewing choices.

Watch questionable shows with your child. Look for opportunities to discuss and evaluate aggressive or violent behaviors. You can ask her questions such as, "Can you think of a better way the Power Rangers could have solved that problem?" "Could that really happen?" "Why do you think there is so much fighting?" You can also help children see the difference between fact and fantasy by saying something like, "In real life, that coyote would not be able to walk after falling off of the cliff."

Good Toys vs. Bad Toys

Play is the most powerful vehicle for young children's learning. When your young child plays, he is exploring and discovering the world around him. Children learn best through direct hands-on experience, and play is the way children do this. If play is your child's work, then toys are his tools. The toys that you provide will directly influence the tone and direction of your child's play. For example, balls and hula hoops will promote active play, and books and puzzles will promote quiet play.

Good toys are safe and age appropriate. They encourage your child to be creative, curious, or cooperative. Good toys will encourage your child to explore and problem solve. Toys that can be played with in many ways are best. These are called open-ended toys and include dolls, blocks, puppets, and Legos.

Bad toys are ones that are very limiting in regard to how a child can play with them. There are not many diverse play themes a child can explore with the "Gomaimem" action figure. Violent toys send violent messages. Toy weapons and violent action figures are among the toys that encourage children to reenact the aggression they see on TV.

Aggression Shaped by Environment

Although it is believed that we are born with the potential for both caring and violence, it is important to note that specific aggressive behavior is influenced and shaped by environment and experiences.

Mommy Knows Best

One year after the FCC deregulated children's TV, seven out of ten of the best-selling toys were connected to a violent children's show. One survey found that 91 percent of teachers report seeing more violent behavior as a result of tie-in marketing of toys and other licensed products.

Do You Have An Aggressive Infant and Toddler?

Your infant's earliest aggressive actions are not intentional. Your infant may grab your face or pull the hair of a playmate. Your child's genuine curiosity and exploration usually cause these behaviors. Your child will not understand how her actions harm another person, so even her rough-and-tumble or playful advances can get out of hand.

Your infant will not understand being punished for these behaviors, but you can take advantage of a teachable moment. Make it clear from the start that aggressive behavior will not be allowed. Even "cute" behaviors such as playful smacks and love bites should be discouraged. Moreover, remember that you are your child's primary role model!

Sometimes your child may accidentally hurt another child or family pet with his "friendly" advances. If this happens, gently stop your child. You can even take his hand to show him how to hug or pet gently while saying, "You are hurting the kitty. Here is how to pet her. See how soft and gentle your touch must be?" Realize that you may need to do this many times.

You can expect your child to display feelings of anger and frustration somewhere between nine and twelve months of age. There are many reasons why children this age will express themselves with aggressive actions.

- They lack the ability to express their emotions or desires with words.
- They have poor impulse control.
- They cannot manage their strong emotions.
- They are egocentric.

Most aggression during the toddler years is instrumental aggression. Toddlers are learning how their behavior can influence someone. Aggressive behavior always gets a reaction, and often it will get the child what she wants: "If I bite Timmy, he will let go of the toy that I want." If your toddler is often hurting others, you may need to make the extra effort to closely supervise her. Stop your child's aggression. Patiently show her how to appropriately express herself with words. You may tell her something like, "Pinching hurts! If you are angry, tell Sylvia, 'Stop, I am mad!'"

Preschool Aggression

As your child approaches preschool age, his ability to tolerate frustration will improve, and he will have stronger language skills and impulse control. Overall, the presence of aggression during temper

Mommy Knows Best

There is a relationship between gender and aggression. Boys do tend to be more aggressive, although it is hard sometimes to determine whether testosterone, cultural acceptance, or media role models has the largest impact.

tantrums should decline as his self-control develops. However, your child may still experience complete meltdowns and possibly hurt others in the process. Try to quickly stop your child's aggression by redirecting or prompting. You can try to encourage him to use words to solve the problem. If all else fails, you will need to remove him from anyone he could hurt. You may need to help him sit in time-out so that he can regain his composure and self-control.

Your preschooler is starting to show an understanding of right and wrong. Early moral development is characterized by decisions that are made according to how their outcome will affect the child. In other words, in the child's eyes, right and acceptable actions are those that help her avoid punishment or gain a reward: "It is wrong to hit the cat because then it will scratch me."

School-Age Aggression

You should expect to see a noticeable decline in aggression from your child by the time he enters school. By now, he should be showing an indication that he is socialized to internalize society's conduct rules and standards. The school-ager is now showing that he has a conscience. His moral thought and decision making are influenced by the opinions of peers and the rules set by authority figures. He would say, "It is wrong to hit the cat because my friends will think I am a bully."

Passive or Proactive: Your Response

Although there are times when it is wise to ignore a tantrum, you must respond promptly when your child is aggressive. You need to make it clear that it is never acceptable to hurt herself or someone else. In contrast, be sure to communicate that you accept your child's feelings. It is okay to be angry, sad, irritated, and so forth. You may say something like, "I can understand why you are angry that you have to come inside, but I will not let you hurt the dog." You may wish to add, "There are better ways to show your anger." (See suggestions for managing destructive behaviors later in this chapter.) This way, you are rejecting the behavior, not your child's feelings.

Punishment is rarely an effective way to respond to aggression. Often, punishment only creates anger and resentment, which may lead to further aggression. Your goal is to use positive discipline to help your child learn appropriate ways to express her strong emotions. You can read more about punishment and discipline in chapter 4.

When your child hurts someone, focus your attention on the victim. This sends the message to

Mommy Must

It is worthwhile to help your child learn the difference between aggressive behavior and assertive behavior. Giving up aggressive behavior does not mean that he has to be passive and give up everything he wants. Assertive behavior means standing up for your own desires and rights while protecting the desires and rights of the other person.

your child that aggression is not an effective way to get what she wants. You can also use this as an opportunity to show your child how her behavior affects someone else: "Can you see that Jacob is crying? He is upset because you took his toy train away from him while he was playing."

When Your Child Hurts Himself

There may be times while your child is having a temper tantrum that he could be at risk for hurting himself. Most of the time, the injury will be unintentional, resulting from flailing on the floor or accidentally hitting himself. It is always a good idea to stay close to younger children when they are having a temper tantrum, to help keep them safe.

Causing Harm on Purpose?

Some young children will intentionally hurt themselves during a temper tantrum. These children become so overwrought with frustration anger that they bite themselves or pull their own hair. If your child is truly hurting herself, you will need to intervene. If you cannot distract or redirect her behavior, then you may need to use the hug hold described above. Be sure to remind your child, "I'm not going to let you hurt yourself."

Additionally, your child may engage in head banging or breath holding. These are also intentional behaviors. These are very dramatic behaviors that your child has learned are effective in getting your attention.

Head Banging

Head banging is a behavior that can occur in children anywhere from nine months to two years of age. Up to 20 percent of all children will bang their heads. Boys are more likely than girls are to engage in this behavior. If you witness your child banging his head, you will understandably be distraught, although most children do not bang their head hard enough to truly hurt themselves. Your instinct will probably be to pick up your child and comfort him to get him to stop. Consequently, you are inadvertently reinforcing the behavior.

Head banging can, on rare occasion, be a symptom of a psychiatric or neurological disorder. It is a good idea to alert your pediatrician when you first observe this behavior. If it is found that your child's head banging is a temper tantrum behavior, then you can work together to find ways to keep your child safe without creating a fuss. Perhaps this means that you

Mindful Mommy

Although rare, sometimes young children will intentionally harm themselves in a calm, more methodical fashion. They may intentionally burn or cut themselves. This behavior is discussed in the next chapter.

will make sure that your child is safe and then ignore him as you would when he is having a full-blown attention-seeking temper tantrum.

A Scary Behavior: Breath Holding

Although also not a harmful behavior, breath holding is perhaps the most frightening common, benign behavior of childhood. Many parents don't realize how common breath holding is. Approximately 5 percent of all children will have breath-holding spells, and they may occur anytime between the ages of one and four. One mother shares, "My son would get angry and just stand and hold his breath. . . . not a sound was coming from him. His lips would turn blue and I would hold him so he would not fall. As soon as he went limp, then he would take a deep breath and begin to scream."

When a child has a breath-holding spell, she will hold her breath until she turns blue and passes out. Some children will also have a small seizure. The good news is that these spells resolve spontaneously. Soon after the child passes out, she will start to breathe, usually within one or two minutes.

Mommy Must
The first time your child has a breath-holding spell, you should take your child to the doctor to rule out any possible physical causes. As with head banging, children can learn to hold their breath for attention. If there is no physical cause, your doctor will probably advise that you try not to reinforce the behavior.

When Your Child Is Destructive

While in the throes of a major temper tantrum, your child may throw or break things. This may be accidental or intentional. As your child is thrashing about, he could easily knock over or hit something. If you predict that your child's temper tantrum will be this out of control, you should secure the area around him as much as you can.

There are times when you may see your child being intentionally destructive. Perhaps he is marking walls or breaking toys at times when he seems to be emotionally in control, but he may still be acting on strong emotions. If your child is destructive with toys, reconsider their appropriateness for your child's age. It may be that your child is too young, and the toy's complexity is frustrating him. Alternatively, if your child is too old for the toy, he will find it boring.

Many activities can help your child channel his destructive impulses. Here are just a few:

- Shred scraps of paper
- Kick a pillow around
- Pull weeds
- Throw rolled socks into a basket
- Scribble hard on the sidewalk with chalk

The way that you should respond to your child's destructive behavior does not depend on whether you believe your child's actions were intentional or not. With your toddler, try redirection. Show her a more appropriate option. For example, "If you wish to cut with the scissors, use them for cutting paper instead of the baby doll's pretty hair." If your child is older, you can also use logical consequences. This is when you require your child to take responsibility for his actions. If he paints on the table, he must clean it off. If he tears a book, he must repair it with clear Con-Tact paper.

Chapter 11

When to Be Concerned?

DID YOU THINK THAT you were ready for any behavior that your child might throw your way? Did you expect that you would see your child throw some temper tantrums along the way, but wasn't quite sure how bad it could be? Were you surprised to see your child have such intense behavior problems? Does your child's behavior appears to be more extreme and problematic than that of any other child you know? When should you start to worry? Should you be concerned that your child has developmental or conduct problems? These are a lot of questions! Let's look deeper into tantrums that cause parents to worry.

What's Normal, What's Not?

Temper tantrums are a normal behavior that you can expect to see as your child develops. Although you may be concerned that your child's tantrum behavior is not normal, odds are that it is.

Your knowledge of how children behave is probably based, for the most part, on your interactions with your own children. You can reasonably expect that, if you have more than one child, each one will be different. Perhaps your two older children have calm dispositions and rarely had temper tantrums. When your third child displays defiance and a stormier demeanor, it is important to remember that her behavior may still be well within the realm of normal. You may find it helpful if you can objectively gauge what are common expectations of behavior for the age of your child. You can gain a wider and less biased perspective in a few ways.

Keep Your Expectations in Check

The question is not whether you perceive your child's behavior to be normal, but whether it is normal in comparison to that of other children her age. Take time to observe your child when she is playing and interacting with other children her own age. Stand back, watch, listen, and ask yourself these questions:

- Is she generally well liked and accepted by the other children?
- Does she seem to tolerate frustration as well as the other children do?
- Is she equal with the other children in problem solving and conflict resolution?
- Can she manage and control her strong emotions as well as the other children her age do?

If you answer no to any of these items, you may wish to investigate further the root of your child's difficulties.

Other parents with children in the same age range as yours can be a wonderful support and resource. Take time to compare notes and share strategies. You may find that you are not so troubled by your toddler's mealtime meltdowns when you hear that Timmy's mother is dealing with this very same issue! Additionally, Amber's mother may have found a great way to cope with sharing conflicts that will work well for you, too.

You can also gain valuable insight from other sources. Books like the one you are reading now can help you learn what is normal and expected behavior for your child's age and development level. If your child is in school or child care, it may be worthwhile to share your concerns with your child's teacher or provider. He or she may be able to offer valuable insight because he or she will have knowledge of child development theory and your individual child's temperament and behavior.

Mindful Mommy

Even adults will have their forms of temper tantrums from time to time. Toddlerhood is prime time for temper tantrums. You should not see your child's tantrums worsening after the age of four. Five to 10 percent of five- and six-year-olds will still have daily temper tantrums, but both their frequency and intensity should continue to decrease.

Investigate the Intensity Level

If you are still concerned about your child's temper tantrum behavior, look at the intensity of his temper tantrums. As there are many different things that may trigger a temper tantrum in your child, your child will exhibit many different ways of responding. Normally, the intensity of your child's tantrum should reflect the level of his emotions. For example, your child may scream and kick when her favorite new toy falls to the ground and breaks, but you should see less intensity in her response when she drops a cookie and it breaks. What you should not see is a child who often overreacts to the smallest of disappointments and frustration.

If you end up walking on eggshells, awaiting the next trigger that will send your child into a rage, you should be concerned. You also do not want to see your child having atypical emotional responses. For example, if your child often cries when you would expect him to be happy, or laughs or seems joyous when he experiences or sees something sad, you should be concerned.

Additionally, the level of intensity of your child's tantrum will influence your ability to console or comfort her; if you find that you are constantly having difficulty in helping your child regain control, you may have cause for concern. With your intervention, most temper tantrums should wind down within five minutes. You will, on occasion, witness an outburst that lasts longer, but you should not see temper tantrums that frequently last for more than fifteen minutes.

How Many Is Too Many?

The number and frequency of your child's temper tantrums will vary, influenced by factors such as stress and your child's level of maturity. During the toddler years, you may see your child have more than one tantrum in a day. The good news is that the frequency of your child's outbursts should begin to decrease noticeably by the time he is around four years old. Some experts recommend that you should alert your pediatrician if your child never has any temper tantrums at all. At any age, more than three temper tantrums a day, over a period of more than a few days, is not normal.

Aggressiveness Unveiled

Some amount of aggressive behavior is common when your child is having a temper tantrum. While she is struggling with strong feelings of anger and frustration, she may lash out and hurt someone. If you have reason for concern regarding your child's temper tantrums, odds are that aggression plays a role in your concerns. You can learn to identify when your child's aggressive behavior has crossed the line.

There are three basic levels of aggression/violence. The first level is mainly instrumental aggression.

This includes behaviors such as pushing, grabbing, and restraining another child. In the second level, the behavior is more intentional, and you may see your child slap, pinch, kick, or hit. The behaviors associated with the third level are violent and are always cause for concern. These behaviors include choking, hitting with an object, using weapons, and not stopping when the victim protests.

Although the focus here is on aggressive behaviors that occur during temper tantrums, there are other signs that can indicate to you that your child has an ongoing or potential problem with violence. If your child gets in lots of fights or your child threatens or intimidates children who are younger or weaker, you should be concerned. When there is a problem, child care providers, teachers, or other parents will often complain about your child's aggression. You should be worried if your child is cruel to animals. Your child may act aggressively with little or no provocation and other children will start to avoid or reject your child because of his aggressive behavior.

If your child is overly aggressive or violent, he may show a preoccupation with violence and violent

Mommy Knows Best

Most forms of aggression should decrease over time. Instrumental aggression usually decreases as children mature and gain verbal skills. Intentionally aggressive behaviors should also decrease once your child learns more appropriate ways to resolve conflict and express anger.

content. You may see them depict graphically violent images in their artwork. They may be preoccupied with violent television shows or video games as well. Please note: Some degree of power/superhero play is normal for young children. The key is that you want to see them play and interact with other children in many ways without always resorting to aggression or violent themes.

Behavior to Watch Out for

Temper tantrums alone are usually not alarming or a cause for concern. However, if your child is also exhibiting any of the behaviors described below, it may be wise to seek out a professional evaluation for your child.

Changes in Habits

Stress and emotional upheaval often result in changes in your child's sleep and/or eating habits. You may see a rapid increase or decrease in your child's appetite or eating patterns. One mother shares:

I felt comfortable that my son was adjusting well to day care. He was always eager to go, he never experienced any separation anxiety, and he was enthusiastic to tell me what he did there at the end of the day. After about two weeks at day care, he suddenly stopped eating breakfast. The first day I questioned his health, but he said he felt fine, and his teacher said he ate well at day care. The second day, I chalked it up to fussiness, as he seemed happy and had no other complaints or symptoms. By the end of the week, it became apparent that his appetite had fallen off at dinnertime, too. My son insisted he felt well and that nothing was bothering him. It was only on the following Monday, when I called his day care, that I learned that he was very upset because his favorite teacher had told his class that she would be leaving for a new school.

Nightmares are common in childhood and can be particularly troublesome for the child who has difficulty distinguishing between fact and fantasy. However, if your child's nightmares are becoming more persistent, your child may be under stress and distress.

Watch That Demeanor

Your child may be troubled and may benefit from professional help if you observe changes in her social or emotional demeanor. Has she recently become exceedingly fearful or anxious? Is she exhibiting low self-esteem? Has she become sullen or withdrawn lately? Has she regressed (gone backward) in her behavior or development? For example, your three-year-old suddenly insists on drinking from a bottle, or your seven-year-old begins to wet the bed at night.

Investigating Self-Injury

It is likely that there will be a time that your child will hurt herself. This may occur when she is flailing about on the floor or kicking and swinging at things around her. This is very different from self-injurious behavior. Self-injurious behavior is when your child is deliberately hurting himself without intending to commit suicide. You should alert a doctor or mental health professional if you believe your child is intentionally hurting himself.

Although there are many ways that your child may choose to hurt herself, some behaviors are much more common than others. The top three are:

- Carving or cutting the skin with a sharp object
- Burning or branding with cigarettes or matches
- Biting

Girls are more likely to injure themselves, possibly because they are more likely to turn aggressive impulses inward rather than expressing them openly.

Mindful Mommy

Self-injurious behavior may be difficult for you to detect. Children usually feel shame and embarrassment about the behavior; therefore, they often harm themselves only when they are alone.

Experts believe that the child who self-injures is doing so to release strong emotions and reduce tension. Some children self-injure so that they can feel pain and combat feelings of detachment. Other children may harm themselves due to feelings of worthlessness, hopelessness, or guilt.

Autism and Tantrums, How Do They Relate?

Both public concern and information about autism have grown in the last twenty years. Autism is a developmental disorder. Extreme and uncontrollable temper tantrums are one of the signs of autism. Each child with autism will be affected differently. The range of symptoms and behaviors occurs on a broad spectrum. Some children may be disabled while others may be fully functional and independent.

Most children with autism are diagnosed around age two or three, though diagnoses around and before age two are now being made a little more frequently as a result of the research that has identified preverbal red flags. Social and communicative characteristics

Mindful Mommy

The signs of autism are usually observed in children ages one to three. Fifteen out of every 10,000 children will have this disorder. Boys are four times as likely as girls are to be diagnosed with autism.

that may be red flags for autism in very young infants include lack of eye contact, lack of interest in caregivers during what would ordinarily be considered pleasurable interactions (i.e., feeding), not responding to their name by the first birthday, and lack of early social reciprocity and affective responses to interaction (mirroring movement, affect, facial expression, and vocalizations).

What's Different About Autistic Temper Tantrums?

There are some key ways in which autism temper tantrums are different than normal tantrums. All in all, the autistic child's temper tantrums are more intense than average temper tantrums are, and it will take longer for adults to console the child and help the child to regain control. When an autistic child has a temper tantrum, it is often difficult to identify the cause. Instead of being able to say, "Okay, he is having a meltdown because I won't buy him candy" or "She is having a temper tantrum because she is tired," the reasons for this child's temper tantrum may seem completely arbitrary. Temper tantrums in the autistic child are very unpredictable. There is often no set pattern, characteristics, or responses. The very same trigger may result in various scenarios. One morning, your child may find that his cereal is too soggy and will sob uncontrollably. The next day, your child, again finding soggy cereal, will scream obscenities and throw his cereal bowl across the room.

Watch for These
Communication Difficulties

Although autism manifests itself in many ways, many children with autism will exhibit communication difficulties. Experts recommend that your child be evaluated if you agree with any of the following items:

- Your child does not babble or coo by her first birthday.
- Your child does not gesture or wave by her first birthday.
- Your child has not said his first word by the age of sixteen months.
- Your child has not said a two-word phrase by his second birthday.
- Your child has exhibited a loss or regression of language skills.

Keep in Mind These Other
Indications of Autism

There are a wide range of other behaviors that could possibly indicate that your child is autistic. However, seeing one behavior does not automatically mean that your child has autism. There may be a separate isolated reason for a behavior. For example, one warning sign is diminished eye contact, which may also indicate vision or hearing difficulties.

Autistic children are often withdrawn from others and from their surroundings. Along with diminished eye contact, they may ignore verbal interactions.

Some children show echolalia. That is, rather than responding to what someone says to him, the child echoes it back, often repeating it multiple times. The autistic child may also withdraw physically. She may resist being touched. Additionally, autistic children often have difficulty playing or interacting with other children.

The autistic child may exhibit an extreme version of the adaptability temperament trait. Adaptability is discussed in detail in Chapter 2. Autistic children may be very slow to adapt, insisting on sameness and routine. They react very strongly to any change in their daily life. Something as minor as forgetting to cut the crust off their peanut butter and jelly sandwich may lead to a temper tantrum.

ADD/ADHD and Your Child's Tantrums

Jason is a bundle of energy. He is always on the go, flitting from one activity to another. He has temper tantrums at the drop of a hat, particularly when he is asked to sit still or wait quietly. Does this describe

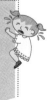

Mindful Mommy

Self-stimulation behaviors (repetitive physical actions) such as rocking, spinning, and head banging are commonly seen in children with autism. However, be aware that these behaviors are also seen in children who are experiencing a lot of stress in their lives.

a child with attention deficit hyperactivity disorder (ADHD) or an average preschool-aged child? It is often difficult to tell, as behaviors associated with ADHD are often normal for young children.

As many as 40 percent of parents will, at some time, suspect that their child has ADHD. The reality is that only 10 percent of children are diagnosed with ADHD. Furthermore, children under the age of six are rarely diagnosed. It is believed the reason for this disparity is due to a heightened awareness of the disorder, along with generally higher parental expectations.

Could Your Child Have ADD/ADHD?

You can have a more objective perspective on whether your child needs to be evaluated for ADHD if you educate yourself about what are reasonable behaviors and expectations for your child's age. It is likely that your child exhibits some of the behaviors described below. What you need to ask yourself is, "Is my child having more difficulty than other children his age?"

A father tells about a morning with his daughter who has ADHD:

She is constantly on the go. This morning was no different. She would barely sit at the table long enough to eat breakfast. Soon afterward, she was upstairs bouncing on her bed. I started up the stairs to remind her that she is not allowed to do that but she met me halfway as she was sliding down the steps on her bottom. She went back up the steps and all was quiet for ten or fifteen minutes. Then I heard some loud banging. When I went to her room, I found her sitting in a pile of yarn and craft materials crying. Over in the corner I could see one of the many projects that she had started tossed in the corner where she had three or four unfinished drawings. "What's wrong, baby?" I asked her. She yelled back at me, "I'm bored, bored, bored!" and she got up and kicked all the yarn under the bed. I sat in the rocker and patted my knee. "Come sit with me," I called. She came over and sat on my lap, but as soon as I tried to put my arm around her, she squirmed off and ran down the steps. By the time I caught up with her, she was doing somersaults over the back of the couch.

Temper tantrums may be common in children with ADD/ADHD as they will often be very impulsive and have difficulty delaying gratification. This may make tasks like waiting for a turn and sharing quite hard. The child with ADD/ADHD may have

Mommy Knows Best

Attention deficit disorder (ADD) generally has two main behavioral components: difficulty paying attention and impulsiveness. When a child with ADD is also hyperactive, he is said to have ADHD.

temper tantrums that last longer than average, but they will usually resolve within twenty to thirty minutes. It is important to note that most misbehaviors on the part of a child with ADHD/ADD are unintentional. For example, she may frequently be destructive, but this comes from careless rather than spiteful actions.

The child with ADHD will have difficulty paying attention. He may have a hard time completing a task, or he may be very careless in finishing a project. He does not pay attention to detail. These children can be observed starting many activities at once without following though on them. Easily distracted, they may leave behind many half-read books and partially built block towers. Being easily distracted also means the child will have a hard time listening, and he will often appear to be forgetful. You may be frustrated with him for always losing things.

Children with ADHD are often very impulsive. They will often interrupt others to add to a conversation. They may want to jump ahead in a line, and they may have a hard time playing a game that requires that they wait for their turn. Your child may have difficulty sitting still. When he must sit still, you will often see him squirm or fidget. He may talk excessively and be always on the move.

At Home with Your ADHD Child

Whether or not your child's pediatrician has chosen to put your child on medication, there are some concrete ways that you can help her manage.

Make a special place for her. Because your child is easily distracted, completed tasks in a timely fashion may prove to be difficult. Set aside a workspace for your child. Remove as many distractions as you can. Have her desk face the wall. Remove the radio and TV from her work area.

Help keep your child on task. You can help your child by prompting him: "Okay, you have folded the socks, now what should you do?" Break down complicated chores or tasks into smaller pieces. Instead of telling him to clean out the garage, give him one small task at a time, such as, "Go and put all the toys in the garage in the big box that is in there. Then report back to me." If your child is a visual learner, try drawing him a diagram for the steps that he needs to take.

Help your child get organized. Children with ADHD often flourish with a lot of structure and routine. It helps them when there is predictability and order in their lives. Help them keep their time organized with to-do lists and calendars. There are many closet organizers and products that you can use to help your child keep her belongs together and organized.

Get her attention. Do not assume that she heard you when you called to her from the backyard. Call her name, get down on her level, and make eye contact before speaking with her.

Let him move. If your child needs to move, give him opportunities to move. If you can, dedicate a space indoors where he can dance or exercise safely, and try to plan outdoor playtime every day, weather permitting. You can add physical activity to everyday activities. Perhaps suggest to your child that he "hop like a bunny" on his way to the bathroom.

Other Behavioral Issues, Beware!

Temper tantrums alone do not indicate that your child has a problem. There are, however, disorders that include temper tantrums as one of the indicators.

Let's Discuss: Oppositional Defiant Disorder

Oppositional defiant disorder (ODD) is sometimes recognized in young children. It is marked by a persistent pattern of behavior where the child is very negative, hostile, and defiant. At least four of the listed signs must be present in your child's behavior for longer than six months in order for your child to be diagnosed with ODD. It is important for you to realize that these behaviors go well beyond the limit-testing behaviors that are typical for toddlers seeking autonomy or for teenagers making a bid for their independence. Here are some of the signs of ODD: argues with adults, often loses his temper, refuses to comply with adult requests or rules, generally angry and resentful, deliberately annoys people, blames others for her mistakes or misbehavior, touchy and easily annoyed by others, often appears spiteful or vindictive.

It is recommended that all adults involved in this child's care and supervision work together. You should all have a system of open communication and present a united front to the child. This is because the child with ODD will often blame others (including other adults) for her behavior. Agree how each problem will be handled in advance so that you are prepared to react in a calm, unemotional fashion.

If you suspect that your child has ODD, you should contact your pediatrician. In the meantime, what seems to work best for these children is a form of behavior modification. Simply put, this means that you will focus on, recognize, and reinforce the positive behaviors that your child engages in. You can set up a reward or token system as explained earlier.

Beware of Signs for Bipolar Disorder

Bipolar disorder, sometimes also called manic depression, is identified in children who exhibit extreme and sometimes rapid changes in mood, energy, thinking, or behavior.

In general, the child with bipolar disorder will appear very moody, swinging between bouts of depression and mania, a state of heightened mood and energy. The bipolar child may be very impulsive at times. Sometimes she will be very motivated and eager, while at other times she will be lethargic and apathetic. The child with bipolar disorder may have explosive temper tantrums, and she may be prone to strong separation anxiety. Tantrums may be particularly intense when the child is in a manic state, as the child is releasing both physical and emotional energy. Bipolar tantrums can last for hours, and some children will lose their memory of having had them. These tantrums will be even more trying for you than a normal tantrum would be. Keep in mind that there is a reason why your child is having such difficulty controlling her emotions and behavior. Your own calm and patience will go a long way toward calming the storm.

Appendix A

Further Resources

Books for Young Children

Adoff, Arnold. *Black is Brown Is Tan.* (Harper & Row, 1992).

Agassi, Martine, Heinlen, Marieka (Illustrator). *Hands Are Not for Hitting.* (Free Spirit Publishing, Inc, 2002).

Aliki. *Feelings.* (Mulberry Books, 1985).

Ancona, George. *Helping Out.* (Clarion, 1985)

Bang, Molly. *When Sophie Gets Angry -- Really, Really Angry.* (Scholastic, Inc., 1999).

Berenstain, Stan Berenstain, Jan. *Berenstain Bears Get the Gimmies.* (Random House, Incorporated, 1988).

Breeze, L. Morris, A. *This Little Baby's Bedtime.* (Little Brown, 1990).

Brown, Tricia. *Someone Special, Just Like You*. (Henry Hulton, 1991).

Carlson, Nancy. *How to Lose All Your Friends*. (Puffin.1977).

Clifton, L. *My Friend Jacob*. (Elsevier/Dutton, 1980).

Crary, Elizabeth, Megale, Marina (Illustrator). *I Want It*. (Parenting Pr., Inc. 1996).

Crary, Elizabeth, Whitney Jean (Illustrator). *I'm Frustrated (Dealing with Feelings Series)*. (Parenting Pr., Inc., 1992).

Emberley Ed E., Miranda Anne (Illustrator). *Glad Monster, Sad Monster: A Book about Feelings*. (Little, Brown & Company, 1997).

Everitt, Betsy. *Mean Soup*. (Harcourt Brace & Company,1995).

Fassler, J. *Howie Helps Himself*. (Whitman, 1975).

Formby, Caroline. *Tristan's Temper Tantrum*. (Child's Play International, Ltd., 1996).

Fox, Mem. *Harriet, You'll Drive Me Wild!*. (Harcourt Children's Books, 2000).

French, Vivian, Elgar Rebecca (Illustrator). *Tiger and the Temper Tantrum*. (Houghton Mifflin Company, 1999).

Kingsley, Emily Perl. *I Can Do It Myself.* (Western Publishing Co. Inc., 1980).

Lachner, Dorothea, Thong Khing (Illustrator). *Andrew's Angry Words*. (North-South Books, 1997).

Little, Lessie Jone, Greenfield, Eloise. *I Can Do It By Myself.* (Thomas Y. Crowell, 1978).

Mayer, Mercer. *There's a Nightmare in My Closet*. (Puffin Books. 1976).

Miller, Margaret. *Baby Faces*. (Simon & Schuster. 1998).

Minarik, Else Homelund, Maurice Sendak (Illustrator). *No Fighting No Biting*. (Harper Trophy, 1978).

Parr, Todd. *Feelings Book*. (Little, Brown & Company, 2000).

Preston, Edna Mitchel. *The Temper Tantrum Book*. (Penguin Putnam Books for Young Readers, 1971).

Spelman, Cornelia, Maude. *When I Feel Angry.* (Albert Whitman, 2000).Spier, Peter. People. (Doubleday, 1980).

Steptoe, John. *Daddy is a Monster . . . Sometimes.* (Harper & Row, 1983).

Stevenson, Harvey (Illustrator). *The Chocolate-Covered-Cookie Tantrum.* (Houghton Mifflin Company, 1999).

Viorst, Judith. *Good-Bye Book.* (Simon & Schuster, 1992).

Books for Older Children

Anderson, Penny S. Siculan, Dan (Illustrator). *Feeling Frustrated.* (Scholastic Library publishing, 1983).

Anfousse, Ginette. *Arthur Throws a Tantrum.* (Formac Publishing Company, Limited, 1993).

Brown, Marc. *How to Be a Friend: A Guide to Making Friends and Keeping Them.*(Little, Brown, 2001).

Burnett. Karen Gedig Burnett. *Simon's Hook: A Story about Teases and Put Downs.* (G R Publishing. 1999).

Cohen-Posey, Kate Lampe, Betsy A. (Illustrator). *How to Handle Bullies, Teasers and Other Meanies: A Book That Takes the Nuisance out of Name Calling and Other Nonsense.* (Rainbow Books, 1995).

Crary, Elizabeth, Whitney, Jean (Illustrator). *I'm Frustrated (Dealing with Feelings Series).* (Parenting Pr., Inc., 1992).

Kay, Barbara, Polland, Kay, Deroy, Craig (Illustrator). *We Can Work It Out: Conflict Resolution for Children.* (Ten Speed Press, 2000).

Lori Lite, Hartigan, Meg (Illustrator). *Boy and a Bear: The Children's Relaxation Book.* (Specialty Press, Incorporated, 1996).

Lichtenheld, Tom. *What Are You So Grumpy About?* (Little, Brown, 2003).

Madison, Lynda, Bendell, Norm (Illustrator). *Feelings Book: The Care and Keeping of Your Emotions.* (Pleasant Company Publications, 2002).

McDonald, Megan. *The Judy Moody Mood Journal.* (Candlewick Press, 2003).

Moser, Adolph. *Don't Rant and Rave on Wednesdays!: The Children's Anger-Control Book.* (Landmark Editions, Inc., 1994).

Romain, Trevor. *Cliques, Phonies, and Other Baloney.* (Free Spirit Publishing, Inc.1998).

Spinelli, Jerry. *Loser* (HarperCollins Publishers, 2003).

Verdick Elizabeth, Lisovskis, Marjorie. *How to Take the Grrrr out of Anger.* (Free Spirit publishing, Inc,) 2002.

Webster-Doyle, Terrence. Why Is Everybody Always Picking on Me?: A Guide to Understanding Bullies for Young People. (Weatherhill, Inc., 1999).

Books for Parents
Bailey, Becky A. Ph.D. *Easy to Love, Difficult to Discipline.* (Morrow & Co., 2000).

Barnes, Robert.G. *Who's in Charge Here?: Overcoming Power Struggles With Your Kids.* (Word Publishing,1990).

Bates Ames, Louise L. Ilg, Frances, Haber, Carol C. *Your Two Year Old: Terrible or Tender.* (Dell publishing Company, Incorporated, 1997).

Bettelheim, Bruno. *Love is Not Enough.* (Avon Books, 1950).

Bowlby, John. *Attachment and Loss Vol.1 Attachment.* (Basic Books, 1969).

Brazelton, T. Berry. *Touchpoints: Your Child's emotional and Behavioral Development.* (Addison-Wesley, 1992).

Craig, Judi, Ph.D. *Parents on the Spot: What to Do When Kids Put Your There.* (Hearst Books, 1994).

Cuthbertson, J. & Schevill, S. *Helping Your Child Sleep through the Night.* (Doubleday, 1985).

Dobson, James C. *Strong-Willed Child.* (Tyndale House, 1992).

Eisenberg, Arlene, Markoff, Heidi E, Hathaway, Sandee. *What to Expect the Toddler Years.* (Workman Publishers, 1994).

Gree, Christopher MD. *Toddler Taming.* (Ballantine Books, 1985).

Karp, Harvey. *The Happiest Toddler on the Block: The New Way to Stop the Daily Battle of Wills and Raise a Secure and Well-Behaved One- to Four-Year-Old.* (Bantam Doubleday Dell Publishing Group, 2004).

Jordan, Timothy J. MD. *Food Fights and Bedtime Battles: A Working Parents Guide to Negotiating Daily Power Struggles.* (Berkley Pub Group,2001).

Kelly, Jeffery MD. *Solving Your Child's Behavior Problems, An Everyday Guide for Parents.* (Little, Brown, 1983).

Kurcinka, Mary S. *Raising Your Spirited Child: A Guide for Parents Whose Child Is More Intense, Sensitive, Perceptive, Persistent, Energetic.* (HarperCollins, 1991).

Kurcinka, Mary Sheedy. *Kids, Parents, and Power Struggles: Winning for a Lifetime.* (HarperCollins, 2001).

Laforge, Ann E. *Tantrums: Secrets to Calming the Storm.* (Simon & Schuster, 996).

Margulis, Jennifer (Editor). *Toddler: Real-life Stories of Those Fickle, Irrational, Urgent, Tiny People We Love.* (Seal Press WA, 2003).

Mitchell, Grace Dewsnap, Lois. *Help! What Do I Do about-- ?: --Biting, Tantrums, and 47 Other Everyday Problems* (Scholastic, Inc, 1994).

Mountrose, Phillip. *Getting Thru to Kids: Problem Solving With Children Ages 6 to 18.* (Holistic Communications, 1991).

Neugebauer, Bonnie. Ed. *Alike and Different: Exploring Our Humanity with Young Children.* (Exchange Press, 1992).

Pruett, Kyle D. *Me, Myself and I: How Children Build Their Sense of Self: 18 to 36 Months.* (Goddard Press, Inc, 1999)

Nelsen, Jane Ed.D. Erwin, Cheryl Duffy, Roslyn. *Positive Discipline: The First Three Years: From Infant To Toddler - Laying The Foundation For Raising A Capable, Confident Child.* (Crown Publishing Group, 1998).

Remboldt, Carole. *Helping Kids Resolve Conflicts Without Violence.* (Johnson Institute Resources for Parents). (Johnson Inst.; 1996).

Rosemond, John K. *Making the "Terrible" Two's Terrific!.* (Andrews McMeel Publishing, 1993).

Sears, William, Sears, Martha. *The Discipline Book.* (Little Brown, 1997).

Shure, Myrna B. *Raising a Thinking Child: Help Your Young Child to Resolve Everyday Conflicts and Get Along With Others: The "I" Can Problem Solve" Program.* (Picket Books, 1996).

Stern, Daniel. *The First Relationship: Infants and Mother.* (Harvard University Press 1977).

Thomas, A. Chess, S. *Temperament and Development*. (Brunner/Mazel, 1977).

Turecki, Stanley, MD., Turner, Leslie. *The Difficult Child*. (Bantam, 1989).

Warwick, Pudney, Whitehouse, Eliane. *A Volcano in My Tummy: Helping children to Handle Anger: A Resources Book for Parents, Caregivers and Teachers*. (Now Society Publishers, 1996).

Williamson, P. *Good Kids. Bad Behavior, Helping Children Learn Self-Discipline*. (Simon & Schuster, 1990).

White, Burton L. *Raising a Happy Unspoiled Child*. (Simon & Schuster, 1994).

Videos for Parents
1,2,3,4 Parents! Video Library, Volume 3: *Building Better Behavior* (2003). Active Parenting Publishers, 1955 Vaughn Rd. NW, Suite 108, Kennesaw, GA 30144-7808, 800-825-0060.

1-2-3 Magic—Managing Difficult Behavior in Children 2-12 (1990). Child Management Inc.

How To Behave So Your Children Will, Too! (2000). Tapeworm Video.

Begin With Love (2002). Civitas Video.

Web Sites for Parents

Dr.Greene.com

Dr. Greene answers questions about behavior development and more, Browse through his articles or join him in a scheduled chat.

www.drgreene.com

AskDr.Sears.com

On this web site you will find information about feeding and sleep problems, childhood illness, along with sound parenting advice.

www.askdrsears.com

PositiveDiscpline.com

This is the place for tons of resources, book excerpts, and articles.

www.positivediscipline.com

Kids Health

KidsHealth has separate areas for kids, teens, and parents

www.kidshealth.org/parent/

Babycenter.com

A huge site! You will find tools, articles, an online store, chats, and a message board

www.babycenter.com

Parenthood.com

Information on development through the life span.

www.parenting.parenthood.com/toddler.html

Parenting: Babies & Toddlers
Check out the tons of links, articles, and discussion board
http://babyparenting.about.com

A Child's Development Calendar
Read all about your child and their accomplishments at each stage of development.
www.vtnea.org/vtnea14.htm

The National Parenting Center
This wonderful site includes articles from many experts and also includes product recall information.
www.tnpc.com

Positive Parenting.com
A huge site with its own bookstore and newsletter.
www.positiveparenting.com

Amazingmoms.com
You can spend a week on this site exploring all the tips, recipes and articles about child development and family life.
www.amazingmoms.com

Support Groups and Organizations

American Academy of Pediatrics
The American Academy of Pediatrics (AAP) is dedicated to providing resources for the health, safety and well being of infants, children, adolescents and young adults.
www.aap.org

Attachment Parenting International
Resources and information to learn more about this parenting style that stresses secure attachment and bonding.

2906 Berry Hill Drive
Nashville, TN 37204
615-298-4334 phone
615-298-9723 fax

Because I Love You
This is a Non-profit organization dedicated to supporting parents with troubled children of any age.
www.becauseiloveyou.org

Children and Adults with Attention-Deficit/ Hyperactivity Disorder (CHADD)

(CHADD) is a national non-profit providing support and information for both children and adults.
8181 Professional Place, Suite 150
Landover, MD 20785

Council for Children with Behavioral Disorders

The Council for Children with Behavioral Disorders (CCBD) is dedicated to promoting and facilitating the education and general welfare of children and youth with behavioral and emotional disorders
Council for Exceptional Children
1920 Association Drive
Reston, VA 20191-1589
703-620-3660 phone
1-888-232-7733 phone
703-264-9494 Fax
www.cec.sped.org

I Am Your Child

This Web site has a wealth of information on parenting and development.
www.yourchild.yahoo.com

MOMS Club International

Over 1,500 chapters with more than 75,000 members in seven countries. Check out their website to find a chapter in area.
www.momsclub.org

Mothers of Preschoolers (MOPS)

International and diverse support network of mothers of preschool children.
MOPS International
2370 South Trenton Way
Denver, CO 80231-3822
303-733-5353 phone
www.gospelcom.net/mops

National Black Child Development Institute (NBCDI)

NBCDI was founded to promote and protect the well being of all African American children.
www.nbcdi.org

National Institute of Child Health and Human Development

This agency is committed to health and welfare of mothers and young children.
www.nichd.nih.gov

Parents as Teachers

PAT is an international early childhood parent education and family support program for families with children ages 0–5.
314-432-4330 Phone
www.patnc.org

Parents & Teachers of Explosive Kids
P.T.E.K. is a non-profit organization that provides support for parents and teachers involved in the care of behaviorally challenging children.
Beth Edelstein
4 Russett Lane
Andover, MA 01810
www.explosivekids.org

Parents Without Partners
An International, non-profit, organization for single parents and their children.
Parents Without Partners, Inc.
1650 South Dixie Highway, Suite 510
Boca Raton, FL 33432
www.parentswithoutpartners.org

Sensory Integration International
A clearinghouse of information and resources for children with sensory integration difficulties.
1602 Cabrillo Ave.
Torrance, CA USA 90501-2812

Zero to Three
Zero to Three is a national non-profit organization committed to examining best practices and polices for young children.
www.zerotothree.org

Appendix C

Glossary

Adaptability
The ability to adapt or change one's behavior in response to the environment.

Adolescence
The teen age years, typically between twelve and eighteen years of age.

Aggression
Behavior that inflicts physical or emotional harm on someone or something else.

Ambivalent Attachment
A lack of a secure bond with the caregiver that results in the child becoming lonely, insecure or withdrawn.

Assertiveness
A way of interacting with others that makes sure that your own needs and desires are met without harming anyone.

Attachment
A close and secure relationship between a child and their primary caregiver.

Attention Deficit Hyperactivity Disorder (ADHD)
Attention Deficit Disorder (ADD) generally has two main behavioral components: difficulty paying attention and impulsiveness. When a child is also hyperactive, then they are said to have ADHD.

Authoritarian
A parenting style where the parent has full control. This style is often harsh and punitive.

Authoritative
A parenting style where the parent has most of the control, but children's input and opinions are respected.

Autism
Autism is a broad-spectrum developmental disorder.

Autonomy
A feeling of independence, the ability to make independent choices and take independent action.

Behavior Modification
Attempting to change or modify a child's behavior by the controlled use of tokens or rewards to reinforce positive behavior.

Bi-polar Disorder
Bipolar disorder is sometimes also called manic depression and identified in children who exhibit extreme and sometimes rapid changes in mood, energy, thinking or behavior.

Bonding
The process of forming an attachment or relationship between two people.

Cognitive Development
Referring to the development of mental or intellectual processes. Cognitive development includes language, problem solving and memory.

Collective Monologue
A conversation where two are more people are speaking but no one seems to be listening or responding to the other person.

Consequences
The direct result of a behavior. If I do THIS, than THIS will happen.

Defiance
Willful or intentional opposition.

Discipline
To guide or teach someone, usually referring to helping a child learn safe behavior and self-control.

Displaced Aggression
Aggression that is aimed at someone or something that was not the original cause of anger or frustration.

Echoholia
Seen in autistic children, this is when they repeatedly echo back what is said to them.

Egocentric
The perception of a young child where they can only see the world through their own eyes and cannot understand anyone else's viewpoint. The egocentric child sees themselves as the center of the world.

Empathy
The ability to see and understand another person's viewpoint or feelings as if you are experiencing it yourself.

Enuresis
Bedwetting. It is common in children through the age of five.

Expressive Language
Language used for expression. Speaking and writing are forms of expressive language.

External Gestation
A time when you carry your infant close to your body, and allow your child to hear your heartbeat and voice and feel constant closeness and touch.

Food jag
A period of time where the child becomes very picky and will only eat one thing, or just a few things.

Gratification
Having one's needs or desires met.

Hyperactive
To be restless, fidgety or easily distracted.

"I" Messages
A positive statement that directly communicates the speaker's wishes or needs. This statement always starts with the word "I." For example, "I wish that you would stop fussing and clean up your room."

Imitation
A mode of learning, where the child observes and model and they consequences of their actions.

Impulsive
The tendency to act without first considering the consequences. Too look before you leap.

Infant
A child between birth and one year of age.

Insecure Attachment
A lack of a secure bond with the caregiver that results in the child being clingy, and craving attention or approval.

Instrumental Aggression

Aggressive behavior that is goal directed, such as pushing someone out of the way so that you can get a seat on the bus.

Intrinsic Motivation

Motivation or action that is not influenced by external consequences or rewards. To do something because of your conscience.

Learned Helplessness

The loss of motivation to try or attempt a new skill or activity, sure that you will only fail anyhow.

Model

To provide an example. Someone who is imitated: role model.

Motherese

Also know as parentese. Motherese is a universal style of speech that adults unconsciously adopt when they are speaking to infants. When they use Motherese, they talk in a high-pitched voice, speak slowly, and use repetition and exaggeration of sounds.

Motivation

A driving force on behavior. People are usually motivated to get their needs met.

Night Terror

A phenomenon that occurs in young children. Unlike nightmares, night terrors occur while the child is in a deep sleep. Although children may scream or cry, they are not fully awake and do not recall the incident when do awaken.

Nurture

To care for someone. Someone who is nurturing is loving, warm and responsive.

Objective Morality

Described by psychologist Jean Piaget, it is the view that your child judges good or bad behavior based upon the result of the action rather than the motivation.

Object Permanence

The understanding that something or someone still exists even when you cannot see or hear it.

Oppositional Defiant Disorder (ODD)

This disorder is marked by a persistent pattern of behavior where the child is very negative, hostile and defiant.

Peer Group

Other people in your same age range or generation.

Permissive

A style of parenting where the parents take very little control. Very few limits are set on children's behavior. Moreover, existing limits are poorly enforced.

Propioceptive System

Refers to your child's awareness of their body and its location in space.

Preschooler

A child between the ages of three and six years of age.

Punishment

A negative response to child's behavior; designed to stop the behavior. There are three main types of punishment: Consequential punishments, verbal punishments and physical punishments.

Receptive Language

Language used for receiving information. Listening and reading are forms of receptive language.

Redirection

A discipline technique where you guide the child to change their behavior to a more appropriate alternative.

Reflective Listening

A statement that shows that you are aware of the other person's concerns, feelings, or interests. For example,

"I can see that you are very upset, but I need you to cleanup your room before you can outside to play."

Reinforcement
The result of an action. A positive consequence to a behavior will increase the likelihood your child will repeat the behavior in hope they will achieve the desired result. Conversely, a negative result will increase the likelihood your child will stop the behavior to avoid the negative consequence.

Scaffolding
When you give your child support and guidance to move on to the next step of complexity.

Secure Attachment
When a child has a bond with their primary caregiver that allows them to be well adjusted, trusting, secure and confident.

Self-Control
The ability to independently recognize, interpret, and display emotion in an appropriate fashion.

Self-Injurious Behavior
When your child is deliberately hurting themselves without intending to commit suicide. Common self-injurious behaviors include cutting, burning and biting.

Self-stimulation

Repetitive physical actions such as rocking, spinning and head banging. Sometimes self-stimulation behaviors are a sign of stress or autism.

Sensory Integration Disorder (SID)

A child with Sensory Integration Disorder has insufficient neurological processing of sensory information. They may be over or under sensitive to different types of sensory information and they can often misinterpret mild sensory signals to perceive them with great discomfort.

Separation Anxiety

The display of anxious behavior when a child is being separated from someone with whom they have formed an attachment. This may occur anywhere from ages 10 months to 4 years of age.

Stranger Anxiety

A display of anxious behavior that an infant will show toward people when they begin to realize that the other person is not their mother or primary caregiver.

Tactile System

The sensory system the guides how we perceive light touch, pressure, pain or temperature.

Temperament

Temperament is your child's inborn disposition. Your child's temperament is his characteristic way of responding and reacting to events and his environment.

Temper Tantrum

A temper tantrum is essentially an uncontrolled outburst of emotion. Temper tantrums are sometimes referred to as fits or meltdowns, and are a common behavior during childhood.

Transitional Object

Any object that a child uses as a security object to help them with separation anxiety. The object often symbolizes a tie to home, mother, or security. Common transitional objects include: blankets and teddy bears.

Toddler

A child between the age of one and three years old.

Token

An object of mark the represents a reward. Tokens such as stickers or chips are often used as part of a reward system.

Vestibular System

This system effects the inner ear and affects their ability to detect their own movement and sense of balance.

Index

Mommy RESCUE Guides

Mommy RESCUE Guide
Breastfeeding

Lifesaving Techniques and Advice for Every Stage of Nursing

Suzanne Fredregill, Certified Breastfeeding Educator

ISBN 10: 1-59869-332-8
ISBN 13: 978-1-59869-332-4
$9.95

Mommy RESCUE Guide
Getting Your Baby to Sleep

Lifesaving Techniques and Advice So You Can Rest, Too

Cynthia MacGregor

ISBN 10: 1-59869-334-4
ISBN 13: 978-1-59869-334-8
$9.95

Mommy RESCUE Guide
Potty Training

Lifesaving Techniques and Advice for an Easy Transition

Linda Sonna, Ph.D.

ISBN 10: 1-59869-333-6
ISBN 13: 978-1-59869-333-1
$9.95

Mommy RESCUE Guide
Toddler Meals

Lifesaving Recipes and Advice for Making Fun, Nutritious Food

Shana Priwer and Cynthia Phillips

ISBN 10: 1-59869-331-X
ISBN 13: 978-1-59869-331-7
$9.95

Mommy RESCUE Guide
Tantrums

Lifesaving Techniques and Advice for Coping When Your Child Can't

Joni Levine, M.Ed.

ISBN 10: 1-59869-598-3
ISBN 13: 978-1-59869-598-4
$9.95

Mommy RESCUE Guide
Twins, Triplets, and More

Lifesaving Techniques and Advice for Surviving Life with Multiples

Pamela Fierro

ISBN 10: 1-59869-688-2
ISBN 13: 978-1-59869-688-2
$9.95

Available wherever books are sold!
Or call 1-800-258-0929 or visit us at *www.adamsmediastore.com*.